THE COMPANY YOU KEEP

THE COMPANY YOU KEEP

Crafting Your Personal & Social Circles for Spiritual Elevation

NIKKI HOOD CSLRC

Envoyai Magazine

To the invaluable lessons borne from overcoming adversity, and to the authentic friendships that emerge,
and flourish, from this profound journey of self-growth.
May we all find the strength to rise, evolve, and celebrate the bonds that shape our destiny.

Chapters

Introduction

In the intricate dance of life, we seldom waltz solo. The friends, mentors, partners, and colleagues we gather around us serve as our choreographers and co-dancers. They influence not only the steps we take but also the rhythm and direction of our dance. Ancient scriptures frequently emphasize the transformative power of companionship, alerting us to the undeniable influence of those we choose to let close. These teachings guide us to be discerning, urging us to see that our associations can either be the music that elevates our dance or the missteps that derail it.

Supportive Scripture

1. *Proverbs 13:20 (NIV):* "Whoever walks with the wise becomes wise, but the companion of fools will suffer harm." **This timeless wisdom accentuates the cascading effect of surrounding oneself with sagacity.**

2. *1 Corinthians 15:33 (NIV):* "'Do not be deceived: 'Bad company ruins good morals.'" **This scripture is a clarion call, underlining the subtle yet continuous influence of our surroundings on our character.**

3. *Sirach 6:14 (NRSV):* "A loyal friend is a powerful defense; those who found one, found a treasure." **Here, the depth and importance of genuine and positive friendship is equated with a treasure - priceless and rare.**

Self-reflection

1. **Circle Check:** Reflect on the main individuals in your life. Do their vibes elevate your spirit? Do their words and actions spur growth and a brighter outlook?

1. **Emotional Barometer:** Recall the exchanges from the last week. Identify the moments that sparked joy and those that felt draining. What recurring themes can you identify?

1. **Mirror Reflection:** While we assess the influence others have on us, we must also introspect on the influence we exert. If your friends were to define the kind of influence you have on them, what might they say?

1. **Wisdom Quest:** Contemplate on someone you view as profoundly wise. What attributes stand out? How can you infuse more of such wisdom into your life, either by association or by personal development?

1. **Relationship Renovation:** Are there certain relationships that need attention, be it healing or nurturing? How can you steer these relationships toward positivity and mutual growth?

Our associations shape our worldview, emotional health, and even our aspirations. Let's remain conscious and intentional about those we invite into our dance of life. After all, a dance is as much about the co-dancers as it is about the individual steps. As you read on, be prepared to explore, introspect, and potentially redefine "the company you keep".

I

FINDING MENTORS AND ROLE MODELS

Identifying Your Goals

Goals are the North Star of our life's voyage, guiding us toward our desired destination and lending purpose to our journey. In the quest for fulfillment and meaning, it's crucial to identify and articulate these aspirations. Whether they relate to personal growth, professional advancement, or spiritual deepening, clear goals empower us to navigate life's challenges with clarity and conviction. Scriptures from various traditions emphasize the importance of vision, purpose, and steadfast pursuit, shedding light on the journey of goal setting and attainment.

Supportive Scriptures

1. ***Proverbs 29:18 (KJV):*** "Where there is no vision, the people perish." **This timeless wisdom accentuates the necessity of having a clear direction or goal in life to thrive.**

2. ***Philippians 3:13-14 (NIV):*** "Brothers and sisters, I do not consider myself yet to have taken hold of it. But one thing I do: Forgetting what is behind and straining toward what is ahead, I press on toward the goal to win the prize for which God has called me heavenward in Christ Jesus." **Here, the emphasis is on relentless pursuit, focus, and the divine calling inherent in our aspirations.**

3. ***Qur'an 20:114 (Islamic scripture):*** "So high [above all] is Allah, the Sovereign, the Truth. And, [O Muhammad], do not hasten with [recitation of] the Qur'an before its revelation is completed to you, and say, 'My Lord, increase me in knowledge.'" **This verse encourages patience, persistence, and an insatiable quest for knowledge as we set and pursue our goals.**

4. ***Bhagavad Gita 2:47 (Hindu scripture):*** "You have the right to perform your prescribed duties, but you are not entitled to the fruits of your actions." **This teaches detachment from outcomes, focusing instead on sincere effort and righteous action.**

Self-reflection

1. ***Envisioning the Future:*** Visualize where you'd like to be in 5, 10, or 20 years. What does that vision look like in terms of career, relationships, personal growth, and spiritual development?

1. ***Prior Accomplishments:*** Reflect on past goals you've achieved. What strategies and mindsets contributed to those successes?

1. ***Values and Goals:*** Consider your core values. How do your goals align with these fundamental beliefs and principles?

1. ***Barriers and Challenges:*** Think about potential challenges or barriers in achieving your goals. How can you strategize to navigate or overcome them?

1. *Short-Term vs. Long-Term:* Break down your long-term goals into actionable short-term objectives. How do these smaller steps contribute to the larger vision?

1. *Seeking Guidance:* Who in your life can offer insight, mentorship, or advice as you refine and pursue your goals?

1. *Measuring Progress:* How will you track and measure your progress? What benchmarks or milestones can you set along the way?

Identifying and articulating clear goals is akin to drawing a map for a cherished journey. While the terrain might be uncertain and the weather unpredictable, with a defined destination in mind and the guiding light of divine wisdom, the path becomes more navigable. Embrace the process with patience, perseverance, and faith, knowing that every step, however small, is progress toward the realization of your dreams.

Researching Potential Mentors

Throughout history, mentors have played a pivotal role in guiding, nurturing, and illuminating the paths of those eager to learn and grow. They offer wisdom gleaned from experience, provide perspective in times of confusion, and serve as beacons in our journeys of personal and professional development. As we stand on the precipice of seeking guidance, it becomes imperative to research and identify potential mentors who align with our aspirations, values, and goals. Scriptures across cultures highlight the profound significance of seeking knowledge, guidance, and the blessings of meaningful mentorship.

Supportive Scriptures

1. *Proverbs 19:20 (NIV):* "Listen to advice and accept discipline, and at the end you will be counted among the wise." **This passage underscores the importance of seeking and heeding wise counsel.**

2. *Titus 2:3-5 (NIV):* "Likewise, teach the older women to be reverent in the way they live... Then they can urge the younger women..." **This emphasizes the tradition of guidance, from the experienced to the novices, a fundamental tenet of mentorship.**

3. *Qur'an 39:9 (Islamic scripture):* "Is one who is devoutly obedient during periods of the night, prostrating and standing [in prayer], fearing the Hereafter and hoping for the mercy of his Lord, [like one who does not]? Say, 'Are those who know equal to those who do not know?'" **This verse extols the virtues of those with knowledge and implicitly encourages seeking them out.**

4. *Dhammapada (Buddhist scripture) 158:* "One who receives a teaching from another regards that person as a heart's treasure." **This line celebrates the revered bond between mentor and mentee.**

Self-reflection Prompts

1. **Defining Mentorship:** Before diving into research, ponder upon what mentorship means to you. What do you seek in a mentor, and what do you hope to gain from the relationship?

2. *Aligning Values:* Consider your core values and principles. How important is it that your mentor aligns with these, and how might differing values impact the mentorship?

1. *Areas of Growth:* Identify areas in your life — professional, personal, spiritual — where you seek growth. How can a mentor guide you in these realms?

1. *Mentor Qualities:* List the attributes you value most in a potential mentor. Is it their experience, approachability, their ability to challenge you, or something else?

1. *Mentor-Mentee Dynamics:* Reflect on the dynamics of past relationships where guidance was involved. What worked and what didn't? How can these insights inform your current search?

1. *Networking and Recommendations:* Think about your current network. Are there potential mentors within it or individuals who might connect you with suitable mentors?

1. *Open-mindedness:* Consider how open you are to mentorship that challenges your current perspectives and pushes you out of your comfort zone.

As you embark on this voyage of researching potential mentors, remember that this relationship is symbiotic. While mentors offer wisdom, experience, and guidance, mentees bring fresh perspectives, enthusiasm, and a willingness to learn. By meticulously choosing someone who aligns with your aspirations and values, you set the stage for a meaningful journey of mutual growth, respect, and transformative learning.

Approaching & Building Relationships

The art of approaching others and forging meaningful connections is a fundamental human endeavor. From the initial outreach to nurturing deep relationships, each phase is dotted with its challenges and rewards. As we navigate the complex terrains of human interactions, it is vital to approach with respect, genuine interest, and humility. Scriptures from myriad traditions emphasize the virtues of companionship, communication, and mutual understanding, offering profound insights into cultivating meaningful relationships.

Supportive Scriptures

1. *Proverbs 18:24 (NIV):* "A man of many companions may come to ruin, but there is a friend who sticks closer than a brother." **This verse points to the depth and quality of relationships being paramount over sheer numbers.**

2. *Romans 12:10 (NIV):* "Be devoted to one another in love. Honor one another above yourselves." **This underlines the importance of selflessness, respect, and love in nurturing relationships.**

3. *Qur'an 49:13 (Islamic scripture):* "O mankind, indeed We have created you from male and female and made you peoples and tribes that you may know one another." **Here, the emphasis is on understanding, embracing diversity, and forging connections.**

4. *1 Peter 3:8 (NIV):* "Finally, all of you, be like-minded, be sympathetic, love one another, be compassionate and humble." **This passage emphasizes mutual understanding, compassion, and humility as foundational virtues in relationship-building.**

Self-reflection

1. ***First Impressions:*** Think about a time when you made a lasting first impression. What elements contributed to that experience? How can you incorporate them when approaching new individuals?

1. ***Barriers to Connection:*** Reflect on personal barriers or inhibitions you've encountered in the past when forging new relationships. How can you address and overcome these hindrances?

1. ***Authenticity in Interactions:*** Assess your recent interactions. Were they genuine, or were there moments of pretense? How does authenticity (or the lack of it) influence the depth and quality of your relationships?

1. ***Building Trust:*** Consider the attributes and actions that help cultivate trust. Are you embodying these in your relationships?

1. ***Mutual Growth:*** Reflect on relationships where both you and the other person grew personally, professionally, or spiritually. What factors contributed to this mutual evolution?

1. ***Understanding Boundaries:*** Ponder upon past interactions where either your boundaries were crossed, or you may have unintentionally crossed someone else's. How can recognizing and respecting boundaries enrich relationships?

1. ***Consistent Communication:*** Evaluate your communication frequency with close acquaintances. How does regular, meaningful communication foster deeper bonds?

Approaching and building relationships is a dance of mutual respect, understanding, and consistent effort. As we reach out to forge new connections or deepen existing ones, may we be guided by the wisdom of the ages, emphasizing genuine interaction, mutual growth, and the sheer joy of meaningful companionship. With every new relationship, we expand our understanding of the world, of humanity, and of ourselves. Let's cherish and nurture these connections, for they are the very fabric of our shared human experience.

Learning From Their Experiences

To walk alongside someone and witness their experiences, absorbing the wisdom they've garnered from life's highs and lows, is a privilege. As we interact with mentors, guides, elders, or even peers, there is a trove of lessons to be imbibed. The art of listening, discerning, and applying these learnings is akin to standing on the shoulders of giants, allowing us to view horizons previously unseen. Scriptures, in their timeless wisdom, highlight the significance of seeking knowledge, respecting those who impart it, and the profound impact of experience.

Supportive Scriptures

1. *Proverbs 20:15 (NIV):* "Gold there is, and rubies in abundance, but lips that speak knowledge are a rare jewel." **This accentuates the preciousness of experiential wisdom and the value of those who share it.**

2. *Job 32:7 (NIV):* "I thought, 'Age should speak; advanced years should teach wisdom.'" **This underscores the insights and perspectives that come with age and experience.**

3. *Qur'an 16:43 (Islamic scripture):* "And We sent not before you except men to whom We revealed [Our message]. So, ask the people of the message if you do not know." **Encouraging seekers of knowledge to approach and learn from those well-versed in divine teachings.**

4. *1 Timothy 4:12 (NIV):* "Don't let anyone look down on you because you are young, but set an example for the believers in speech, in conduct, in love, in faith and in purity." **This verse emphasizes that wisdom can emerge from youth, urging them to lead by example.**

Self-reflection

1. *Active Listening:* Reflect on a recent interaction where you genuinely listened, without interjecting or formulating a response in your mind. How did this enhance your understanding?

1. *Sifting Through the Stories:* Recall a moment when someone shared a personal experience with you. What underlying lessons or morals did you extract from their narrative?

2. *Applying Learned Lessons:* Think of a piece of advice or a lesson

you've acquired from someone else's experience. How have you incorporated it into your life?

1. *Respect and Gratitude:* Consider the individuals who have opened their lives and experiences for your learning. How do you express gratitude and respect towards them?

1. *Interpreting Relevance:* Not all experiences shared will directly apply to your life. Reflect on how you discern what is relevant and adapt these lessons to your unique path.

1. *The Role of Empathy:* Think about how empathizing with someone's experiences deepens your connection with them and enriches your learning process.

1. *Embracing Diverse Experiences:* Ponder upon the range of experiences you've been exposed to. How has diversity in these narratives broadened your perspective?

Learning from the experiences of others is a journey of humility, reverence, and discernment. As we navigate this pathway, may we be ever attentive, sifting through stories for the pearls of wisdom they contain, and integrating these gems into the mosaic of our own lives. In human experience, every thread, every story, and every lesson adds depth, color, and meaning to the collective whole.

Being a Mentor & Role Model Yourself

Stepping into the role of a mentor is a transformative experience. Beyond the privilege of guiding another, it's an opportunity for introspection, growth, and mutual learning. Becoming a beacon for others requires authenticity, commitment, and a deep-seated desire to make a difference. Scriptures from diverse traditions highlight the virtues of leadership, guiding others, and the profound impact of setting an example.

Supportive Scriptures

1. *Proverbs 27:17 (NIV):* "As iron sharpens iron, so one person sharpens another." **This scripture speaks to the reciprocal growth and refinement that occurs in a mentoring relationship.**

2. *Matthew 5:16 (NIV):* "In the same way, let your light shine before others, that they may see your good deeds and glorify your Father in heaven." **Encouraging individuals to lead by example and inspire others.**

3. *Qur'an 3:110 (Islamic scripture):* "You are the best community raised up for mankind. You enjoin good and forbid evil and you believe in Allah." **Here, there's an emphasis on being role models and guiding communities toward the path of righteousness.**

4. *Philippians 4:9 (NIV):* "Whatever you have learned or received or heard from me or seen in me—put it into practice." **Encouraging emulation of good practices and behaviors witnessed in mentors.**

Self-reflection

1. *Personal Growth Journey:* Reflect on your own journey. What were the lessons, trials, and triumphs that shaped you? How can you share these with others to inspire and guide?

1. ***Attributes of a Mentor:*** Think about the mentors in your life. What attributes and behaviors did you most admire? How can you embody these as you guide others?

1. ***Reciprocal Learning:*** Consider a moment when mentoring someone led to your own learning and growth. How does this mutual exchange of wisdom enrich the mentoring relationship?

1. ***Setting Boundaries:*** As a mentor, how do you establish and maintain boundaries while ensuring accessibility and openness with your mentees?

1. ***Handling Differences:*** Reflect on times when your perspective differed from your mentee's. How did you navigate these differences while maintaining respect and understanding?

1. ***Empowerment Over Dependency:*** Ponder on your approach towards mentoring. Are you empowering individuals to discover and navigate their path or inadvertently fostering dependency?
2. ***Legacy and Impact:*** Look into the future. What legacy or impact do you hope your mentoring will leave behind?

Being a mentor and role model is a sacred responsibility—one that can leave an indelible mark on the canvas of another's life. As you undertake this role, may the guiding light of scriptures and the wisdom of self-reflection steer you toward authenticity, mutual growth, and lasting impact. Remember, as you light the path for another, your own journey is illuminated in ways previously unimagined. Embrace the beauty of this duality and let the journey of mentorship be a blessing for both the guide and the seeker.

2

THE POWER OF POSITIVE CONNECTIONS

The Power of Influence

Throughout the ages, the concept of influence has played a pivotal role in shaping societies, beliefs, and individual destinies. Influence can be as subtle as a whisper or as profound as a battle cry; it is the undercurrent that determines the choices we make, the beliefs we hold dear, and the paths we choose to follow. Sacred scriptures from various traditions have often emphasized the transformative power of influence—both the influence we exert on others and that which we allow others to exert on us.

Supportive Scriptures

1. *Matthew 5:13-16 (NIV):* "You are the salt of the earth... You are the light of the world. A town built on a hill cannot be hidden... In the same way, let your light shine before others, that they may see your good deeds and glorify your Father in heaven." **This scripture underscores our potential to be a positive influence, to be agents of change and light in the world.**

2. *Proverbs 22:24-25 (NIV):* "Do not make friends with a hot-tempered person, do not associate with one easily angered, or

you may learn their ways and get yourself ensnared." **This verse is a cautionary tale on the perils of negative influence.**

3. *Romans 12:2 (NIV):* "Do not conform to the pattern of this world but be transformed by the renewing of your mind." **Here, the emphasis is on discernment, on resisting negative external influences, and cultivating inner strength and wisdom.**

4. *1 Timothy 4:12 (NIV):* "Don't let anyone look down on you because you are young, but set an example for the believers in speech, in conduct, in love, in faith and in purity." **This scripture emphasizes the power of leading by example, regardless of age or stature.**

Self-reflection

1. *Influence Inventory:* Reflect on the individuals or entities (media, books, etc.) that have had the most significant influence on your life. What values or beliefs have they instilled in you?

1. *Guarding the Gates:* Recognizing that our senses are gateways to influence, in what ways can you be more discerning about what you listen to, watch, read, or discuss?

1. *Your Ripple Effect:* Consider a recent decision or action of yours. How did it impact others around you? Were you content with the ripple effect it created?

1. ***Agents of Change:*** Recall a time when you were positively influenced by someone. How can you emulate those qualities to be a force of good for others?

1. ***Shifting Sands:*** Are there areas in your life where you feel swayed by popular opinion, peer pressure, or societal norms? How can you ground yourself in your own truth and values?

Recognizing the power of influence and harnessing it judiciously can be transformative. As we navigate the vast ocean of interactions, opinions, and experiences, may we become beacons of positive influence and, in turn, choose influences that align with our higher self and purpose.

The Company You Keep

In every epoch of history, and across cultures, the essence of human experience has been deeply intertwined with the relationships we cultivate. The people we choose to surround ourselves with—our companions, confidantes, mentors, and friends—can be either a balm to our souls or a source of tumult. As with the tender care a gardener gives to their plants, we must tend to our relationships with discernment and wisdom. Scriptures, as the repositories of age-old wisdom, have long recognized and illuminated the profound impact of the company we keep.

Supportive Scriptures

1. ***Proverbs 27:17 (NIV):*** "As iron sharpens iron, so one person sharpens another." **This scripture underlines the idea that through**

constructive relationships, we hone and refine each other's characters.

2. *1 Corinthians 5:11 (NIV):* "But now I am writing to you that you must not associate with anyone who claims to be a brother or sister but is sexually immoral or greedy... Do not even eat with such people." **This admonition encourages discernment in choosing company, emphasizing the need to distance oneself from those who may lead us astray.**

3. *Psalm 1:1 (NIV):* "Blessed is the one who does not walk in step with the wicked or stand in the way that sinners take or sit in the company of mockers." **The Psalmist highlights the blessings and spiritual well-being that come from consciously avoiding negative influences.**

4. *2 Corinthians 6:14 (NIV):* "Do not be yoked together with unbelievers. For what do righteousness and wickedness have in common? Or what fellowship can light have with darkness?" **This verse emphasizes the importance of aligning with those who share similar values and principles.**

Self-reflection

1. *Circle of Influence:* List the five people you interact with most often. What are the predominant qualities, values, and behaviors they exhibit? How do they align with your own?

1. *Emotional Check:* After spending time with someone, do you often feel uplifted, neutral, or drained? This emotional barometer can be a key indicator of the influence a person has on you.

1. ***Reciprocity in Relationships:*** Reflect on whether you play the role of giver, taker, or equal partner in your relationships. How can you foster a balance, ensuring that you are both supportive and supported?

1. ***Shared Values:*** Think about the core values that are non-negotiable for you. Do the people you spend the most time with uphold these values? If not, how does it impact your relationship?

1. ***Growth and Nourishment:*** Are there relationships in your life that have spurred personal growth? Conversely, are there associations that have stunted your spiritual or emotional development?

The adage, "show me your friends, and I'll show you your future," underscores the significant impact our company has on our journey. As we traverse the labyrinth of life, may we be endowed with the wisdom to choose companions who illuminate our path, challenge us to grow, and walk alongside us with love and integrity.

Recognizing Toxic Relationships

In the intricate dance of human interactions, relationships play a defining role. They have the power to uplift and heal, but they can also hinder and harm. As much as the light of a loving relationship can illuminate our path, the shadows cast by toxic relationships can obscure our journey. Wisdom traditions from across the world acknowledge this delicate balance and offer profound insights to help us navigate the waters of interpersonal dynamics.

Supportive Scriptures

1. *Proverbs 22:24-25 (NIV):* "Do not make friends with a hot-tempered person, do not associate with one easily angered, or you may learn their ways and get yourself ensnared." **This scripture highlights the potential dangers of surrounding ourselves with volatile individuals and how their behaviors can influence us.**

2. *1 Corinthians 15:33 (NIV):* "Do not be misled: 'Bad company corrupts good character.'" **A clear warning about the kind of company we keep and its potential to sway our moral compass.**

3. *Psalm 26:4-5 (NIV):* "I do not sit with the deceitful, nor do I associate with hypocrites. I abhor the assembly of evildoers and refuse to sit with the wicked." **This scripture underlines the importance of being discerning about our associations.**

4. *2 Timothy 3:2-5 (NIV):* "People will be lovers of themselves, lovers of money, boastful, proud, abusive... having a form of godliness but denying its power. Have nothing to do with such people." **An admonition to be wary of those who display outward signs of righteousness but lack genuine spiritual depth.**

Self-reflection

1. *Emotional Well-being:* After spending time with someone, do you feel energized or drained? Continual emotional depletion after interactions can be a sign of a toxic relationship.

1. *Patterns of Disrespect:* Reflect on your interactions with those closest to you. Are there recurring patterns of disrespect, manipulation, or one-sidedness?

1. ***Values and Boundaries:*** Do your relationships respect your personal boundaries and values? Or are they often crossed and disregarded?

1. ***Growth or Stagnation:*** Does the relationship encourage your personal and spiritual growth, or does it feel stagnating and confining?
2. *Inner Voice:* Sometimes, our intuition speaks louder than reason. What is your gut feeling about certain relationships in your life?

1. ***Seeking Counsel:*** Have trusted friends or mentors expressed concerns about certain relationships you maintain? Often, an external perspective can shed light on things we might be too close to see.

Recognizing toxic relationships is an essential step toward ensuring our emotional, mental, and spiritual well-being. The journey may require courage, discernment, and sometimes painful decisions, but the promise of a life filled with genuine, uplifting connections makes the pursuit worthwhile. As we navigate the vast landscape of human relationships, may we be graced with the wisdom to embrace the nourishing and release the toxic, always moving closer to our true selves and the Divine.

Creating a Positive Inner Circle

In our life's journey, one of the most profound choices we make is deciding who to let into our inner sanctum – the close-knit circle of confidants and companions who influence our thoughts, behaviors, and aspirations. This inner circle can be likened to the soil in which a seedling is planted; its quality determines how well the plant will flourish. In seeking spiritual and emotional well-being, creating a positive inner circle is paramount. Sacred texts provide guidance on how to cultivate such enriching environments.

Supportive Scriptures

1. *Proverbs 13:20 (NIV):* "Walk with the wise and become wise, for a companion of fools suffers harm." **This timeless wisdom elucidates the essence of surrounding oneself with those who nurture wisdom.**

2. *Hebrews 10:24-25 (NIV):* "And let us consider how we may spur one another on toward love and good deeds, not giving up meeting together, as some are in the habit of doing, but encouraging one another." **This scripture speaks to the power of collective encouragement and spiritual togetherness.**

3. *Sirach 6:14-16 (Apocrypha):* "Faithful friends are a sturdy shelter: whoever finds one has found a treasure. Faithful friends are beyond price; no amount can balance their worth." **The value of genuine friendships is extolled here, emphasizing their rarity and significance.**

4. *1 Thessalonians 5:11 (NIV):* "Therefore encourage one another and build each other up, just as in fact you are doing." **An exhortation to consistently uplift and support those in our community.**

Self-reflection

1. ***Defining Qualities:*** List down the attributes you desire in the individuals comprising your inner circle. Reflect on why each quality is important to you.

2. ***Present Associations:*** Evaluate your current close relationships. Do they reflect the attributes you've listed? If not, what changes might you consider?

3. ***Seek and Offer Value:*** Reflect on what you bring to your inner circle. Are you uplifting, encouraging, and positive? How can you enhance the value you provide to your close relationships?

4. ***Expanding Your Circle:*** Are there individuals in your broader network whom you feel could positively influence your inner circle? How might you foster deeper connections with them?

5. ***Nurturing the Circle:*** Relationships, like plants, need nurturing. What consistent actions can you take to ensure your inner circle remains positive, supportive, and flourishing?

6. ***Addressing Discord:*** Even the most harmonious groups face challenges. How can you proactively address and resolve discord within your inner circle, ensuring its longevity and health?

To create a positive inner circle is to craft a sanctuary of mutual respect, growth, and love. It is about building a haven where everyone is both a beneficiary and a benefactor, receiving and offering light in equal measure. As we consciously cultivate such circles, may our lives be enriched with joy, wisdom, and an unwavering sense of community, drawing us ever closer to our higher selves and our spiritual aspirations.

The Benefits of Diverse Connections

In the intricate mosaic of humanity, every individual represents a unique tile, holding stories, wisdom, experiences, and perspectives shaped by myriad factors — culture, geography, tradition, and personal journeys. As we weave our life's tapestry, incorporating diverse connections becomes an enriching endeavor. It broadens horizons, challenges viewpoints, and fosters growth. Sacred scriptures from various traditions extol the beauty and value of unity in diversity, urging us to embrace the vastness of the human experience.

Supportive Scriptures

1. *Galatians 3:28 (NIV):* "There is neither Jew nor Gentile, neither slave nor free, nor is there male and female, for you are all one in Christ Jesus." **This scripture celebrates the underlying unity of all humans, transcending superficial divisions.**

2. *Qur'an 49:13 (Islamic scripture):* "O mankind, indeed We have created you from male and female and made you peoples and tribes that you may know one another. Indeed, the most noble of you in the sight of Allah is the most righteous of you." **This verse underscores the beauty of diversity and promotes mutual understanding among different groups.**

3. *Rigveda 1.164.46 (Hindu scripture):* "Truth is One, the wise call it by many names." **This ancient text emphasizes the universality of truth and wisdom, irrespective of the diverse paths that lead to it.**

4. *1 Corinthians 12:12-14 (NIV):* "Just as a body, though one, has many parts, but all its many parts form one body, so it is with Christ. For we were all baptized by one Spirit to form one body—whether Jews or Gentiles, slave or free—and we were all given the one Spirit to drink. Even so, the body is not made up of one part but of many." **This passage celebrates the multiplicity within unity and how every individual has a unique role to play in the larger community.**

Self-reflection

1. ***Expanding Horizons:*** Think about the most diverse relationship or friendship you have. How has this connection broadened your understanding of the world?

1. ***Challenging Perspectives:*** Recall a time when a diverse connection challenged your viewpoint. How did you feel initially, and what was the eventual outcome?

1. ***Cultural Curiosity:*** Are there specific cultures or communities you're curious about? How can you foster connections that help you understand these cultures better?

1. ***Unified in Diversity:*** Reflect on moments when, despite differences, you felt a deep sense of unity and connection with someone from a different background.

1. ***Embracing Differences:*** Consider any biases or prejudices you might unknowingly hold. How can you actively work towards unlearning them and embracing diversity wholeheartedly?

1. ***Gifts of Diversity:*** In what ways has diversity enriched your personal, professional, and spiritual life? How can you be more proactive in seeking diverse connections?

To cultivate diverse connections is to willingly embark on a journey of discovery, understanding, and mutual respect. It's an invitation to revel in the myriad hues of humanity, recognizing that every color adds depth and richness to the collective human experience. As we embrace diversity, may we remember that beneath the tapestry of differences lies a shared essence, an unbreakable bond that makes us inherently human and eternally connected.

3

SURROUNDING YOURSELF WITH LIKE-MINDED INDIVIDUALS

Identifying Your Passions

The flame of passion, when ignited, has the power to transform an ordinary journey into an extraordinary adventure. Passions breathe life into our pursuits, infusing them with purpose and zeal. They are the heartbeat of our souls, guiding us toward what truly resonates with our innermost being. Identifying these passions becomes a pivotal step in crafting a life that is not just lived but also celebrated. Ancient scriptures, spanning diverse traditions, have often touched upon the quest to find one's true calling and the beauty of pursuing it with all one's heart.

Supportive Scriptures

1. ***Psalm 37:4 (NIV):*** "Take delight in the LORD, and he will give you the desires of your heart." **This scripture speaks to aligning one's passions with divine purpose, emphasizing that genuine fulfillment stems from this alignment.**

2. ***Bhagavad Gita 18:46 (Hindu scripture):*** "By worship of the Lord, who is the source of all beings and who is all-pervading, a person can attain perfection through performing his own work." **This**

passage underscores the idea that dedicating one's passions to the divine can lead to true perfection and fulfillment.

3. *Qur'an 62:11 (Islamic scripture):* "But when they saw a transaction or a diversion, [O Muhammad], they rushed to it and left you standing. Say, 'What is with Allah is better than diversion and then a transaction and Allah is the best of providers.'" **This verse hints at the transient nature of worldly passions and the everlasting fulfillment of passions aligned with the divine.**

4. *Colossians 3:23 (NIV):* "Whatever you do, work at it with all your heart, as working for the Lord, not for human masters." **A call to immerse oneself wholeheartedly in one's pursuits, seeing them as a form of divine service.**

Self-reflection

1. *Heart's Whispers:* When you are silent and still, what does your heart yearn for? What activities or pursuits make time fly for you?

1. *Childhood Clues:* Think back to your younger years. Were there activities or interests that always captivated you, pointing towards a latent passion?

1. 3. *Joy and Energy:* What activities or tasks fill you with a burst of energy and happiness, regardless of any external rewards?

1. *Natural Flow:* Are there things you do where everything just seems to 'click', and you find yourself in a state of 'flow'?

1. *Life's Highlights:* Reflect on the moments in life when you felt most alive. What were you doing during those times? What common thread runs through these moments?

1. *The 'Why' Behind Passion:* Why do certain activities resonate with you? Is it the process, the outcome, the impact, or something deeper?

1. *The Intersection:* Where do your skills, interests, and the needs of the world around you intersect? This convergence often points towards a passion that is both fulfilling and impactful.

Identifying our passions is akin to discovering the compass of our souls. It provides direction, purpose, and a deep sense of fulfillment. As we delve into this introspective journey, may we be graced with clarity, courage, and conviction to not just identify our passions, but to pursue them with relentless zeal, lighting up both our paths and those of others we touch along the way.

Joining Communities & Groups

Human beings are innately social creatures, driven by a need to connect, belong, and share experiences. Communities and groups provide an arena where shared passions, purposes, or pursuits create a bond stronger than many other ties. They offer a collective reservoir of knowledge, support, and motivation. Historically, societies thrived on the foundation of communities, be it guilds, tribes, congregations, or forums. Sacred scriptures across cultures emphasize the significance and strength of unity, underscoring the power of community.

Supportive Scriptures

1. *Hebrews 10:24-25 (NIV):* "And let us consider how we may spur one another on toward love and good deeds, not giving up meeting together, as some are in the habit of doing, but encouraging one another." Here, the essence of community — to motivate, inspire, and uplift — is highlighted.

2. *Proverbs 27:17 (NIV):* "As iron sharpens iron, so one person sharpens another." **This wisdom illustrates how community interactions refine and improve us.**

3. *Qur'an 3:103 (Islamic scripture):* "And hold firmly to the rope of Allah all together and do not become divided. And remember the favor of Allah upon you - when you were enemies and He brought your hearts together and you became, by His favor, brothers." **A beautiful reminder of how communities can bridge differences and foster unity.**

4. *1 Corinthians 1:10 (NIV):* "I appeal to you, brothers and sisters, in the name of our Lord Jesus Christ, that all of you agree with one another in what you say and that there be no divisions among you, but that you be perfectly united in mind and thought." **The

verse emphasizes harmony within a community, urging members to work towards unity of purpose and thought.

Self-reflection

1. *Communities of the Past:* Reflect on the groups or communities you've been a part of in the past. What drew you to them, and what were your key takeaways?

1. *Seeking Synergy:* Think about your passions and goals. Are there communities out there that align with them? If not, could you consider starting one?

1. *Role within the Group:* In a community or group setting, what roles naturally resonate with you? Are you a leader, a supporter, a planner, or a participant? How can you leverage this role for the community's benefit?

1. *Learning from Differences:* Every community is a mix of diverse individuals. Reflect on moments when this diversity led to disagreements. How did you handle it? How can you promote understanding and unity in future situations?

1. ***Community versus Individual Goals:*** Sometimes, community objectives might diverge from personal aspirations. How would you balance the two? When would you prioritize one over the other?

1. ***Growth through Community:*** How has being part of a community aided your personal growth? Are there areas of growth you hope to achieve through future community interactions?

Joining communities and groups can be a transformative experience. They are platforms where individual flames come together, forging a blazing fire of collective strength, warmth, and illumination. As we navigate the vast seas of life, may we find solace, strength, and sustenance in our shared journeys within these communities, drawing inspiration and offering it in equal measure.

Nurturing Supportive Friendships

Throughout history, the importance of friendships has been paramount. Supportive friendships, akin to rare treasures, enrich our lives in myriad ways. They provide solace in moments of solitude, strength in times of weakness, and joy amidst life's challenges. A genuine friend can be a beacon of hope, a mirror reflecting our true selves, and a bond that remains unbroken by the tumultuous waves of life. Various scriptures have captured the essence of such profound relationships, illuminating the path of nurturing these bonds.

Supportive Scriptures

1. ***Proverbs 17:17 (NIV):*** "A friend loves at all times, and a brother is born for adversity." **This passage underscores the unwavering**

nature of true friendship, emphasizing its steadfastness in challenging times.

2. *Sirach 6:14-16 (Apocrypha):* "A faithful friend is a sturdy shelter; he who finds one finds a treasure. A faithful friend is beyond price, no sum can balance his worth. A faithful friend is a life-saving remedy, such as he who fears God finds." **The verses beautifully elucidate the invaluable nature of genuine friendships.**

3. *Qur'an 9:71 (Islamic scripture):* "The believing men and believing women are allies of one another. They enjoin what is right and forbid what is wrong..." **This verse emphasizes mutual support, guidance, and shared principles in the realm of friendships.**

4. *1 Thessalonians 5:11 (NIV):* "Therefore encourage one another and build each other up, just as in fact you are doing." **A clarion call to continually uplift and fortify each other in the journey of friendship.**

Self-reflection

1. *Memory Lane:* Reflect on a time when a friend stood by you during a challenging phase. What did that support mean to you? Conversely, think of a moment when you were that pillar for someone else.

1. *Qualities and Values:* Enumerate the qualities you value most in a friend. How do these align with the qualities you bring to your friendships?

1. ***Rekindling Bonds:*** Are there friendships that have waned over time that you wish to rekindle? What steps can you take towards that?

1. ***Setting Boundaries:*** While supportive friendships are crucial, setting healthy boundaries is equally essential. Reflect on any boundaries you may need to set or respect in your friendships.

1. ***Growth and Evolution:*** Consider how you and your close friends have evolved over time. How have these changes impacted your bond?

1. ***Nurturing the Bond:*** Friendships, like plants, need nurturing. What acts or gestures can you incorporate regularly to strengthen your friendships?

1. ***Learning and Adapting:*** Recall a disagreement or conflict with a friend. How did you navigate it? What did you learn, and how can you apply that wisdom to future challenges?

Nurturing supportive friendships is akin to tending a sacred garden. The blossoms of trust, shared memories, laughter, and solace that emerge are rewards for the love, patience, and care invested. As we journey through life, may we cherish these bonds, understand their ephemeral nature yet timeless impact, and strive to be the friend we wish to have by our side.

Collaborating for Success

In our individual journeys, we often encounter crossroads where the solitary path may seem daunting. It is in these moments that the power of collaboration emerges, illuminating the way forward. When two or more individuals unite their strengths, expertise, and visions, they forge a synergy that can catapult them towards success, beyond what they might achieve alone. The beauty of collaboration lies not just in shared triumphs, but in collective learning, mutual growth, and the sheer joy of journeying together. Many scriptures across cultures emphasize the strength of unity and the blessings of collaborative efforts.

Supportive Scripture

1. *Ecclesiastes 4:9-12 (NIV):* "Two are better than one, because they have a good return for their labor: If either of them falls down, one can help the other up. But pity anyone who falls and has no one to help them up... Though one may be overpowered, two can defend themselves. A cord of three strands is not quickly broken." **This passage beautifully captures the strength of collaboration and mutual support.**

2. *1 Corinthians 12:14 (NIV):* "For the body is not one member, but many." **This reminds us that just as a body requires various organs to function harmoniously, success often stems from diverse individuals collaborating seamlessly.**

3. *Qur'an 49:13 (Islamic scripture):* "O mankind, indeed We have created you from male and female and made you peoples and tribes that you may know one another..." **This verse suggests that diversity is divinely ordained for mutual recognition and collaboration.**

4. *Philippians 2:2 (NIV):* "Then make my joy complete by being like-minded, having the same love, being one in spirit and of one mind." **Emphasizing the essence of unity in purpose and vision for effective collaboration.**

Self-reflection

1. *Past Collaborations:* Reflect on an experience where you collaborated with others. What were the successes and challenges of that partnership?

1. *Your Strengths in a Team:* What unique qualities do you bring to a team? How do you see these complementing the skills of others?

1. *Openness to Ideas:* Think of a time when a collaborative decision didn't align with your personal view. How did you navigate this? How might you approach such situations in the future?

1. *Learning from Differences:* Collaboration often brings together diverse perspectives. How can you harness this diversity for creative solutions rather than letting it become a point of contention?

1. ***Building Trust:*** Trust is the foundation of any successful collaboration. Reflect on ways you can cultivate trust within a team or partnership.

1. ***Vision Sharing:*** How can you ensure that all collaborators share a unified vision, while still valuing individual input?

1. ***Feedback and Growth:*** Consider the importance of feedback in collaborative settings. How can you give and receive feedback constructively to foster mutual growth?

Collaboration, when approached with openness, respect, and a shared vision, can be a powerful catalyst for success. It bridges gaps, weaves together strengths, and creates a tapestry of collective triumphs. As we tread the path of collaboration, may we remain rooted in the wisdom of unity, cherishing each contribution and celebrating every shared milestone.

Expanding Your Network

Every single individual is a unique thread, possessing distinctive skills, experiences, and perspectives. When we try to expand our network, we weave our thread into an ever-growing mosaic, making both personal and professional advancements. Expanding one's network isn't merely about quantity; it's about diversifying and enriching our connections, ensuring a mutual flow of value, wisdom, and support. Scriptures from various traditions laud the merits of establishing broader relationships and highlight the blessings that emanate from such connections.

Supportive Scriptures

1. *Proverbs 18:24 (NIV):* "One who has unreliable friends soon comes to ruin, but there is a friend who sticks closer than a brother." **This teaches us the importance of quality over quantity in our relationships, urging discernment as we expand our circles.**

2. *Romans 12:4-5 (NIV):* "For just as each of us has one body with many members, and these members do not all have the same function, so in Christ we, though many, form one body, and each member belongs to all the others." **This underlines the importance of diversity in any network, emphasizing the collective strength derived from individual uniqueness.**

3. *Qur'an 49:11 (Islamic scripture):* "O you who have believed, let not a people ridicule [another] people; perhaps they may be better than them..." **This verse encourages us to be open-minded and respectful towards all, recognizing the potential value in every individual we encounter.**

4. *Luke 6:38 (NIV):* "Give, and it will be given to you. A good measure, pressed down, shaken together and running over, will be poured into your lap." **This highlights the principle of reciprocity in networking — the more value and support we offer, the more we receive in return.**

Self-reflection

1. *Current Network Evaluation:* Reflect on the current state of your network. Which connections inspire, challenge, and support you?

1. *Networking Intent:* As you seek to expand your network, what are your core intentions? Are you seeking mentorship, collaboration, diverse perspectives, or simply broader horizons?

2. ***Giving Back:*** Networking isn't a one-way street. How can you offer value, assistance, or support within your network?

1. ***Diversity in Connections:*** How diverse is your current network in terms of age, profession, culture, and perspectives? How can you enrich this diversity?

1. ***Genuine Engagement:*** Think of a recent networking interaction that felt genuinely enriching. What made it stand out? How can you ensure such authenticity in future interactions?

1. ***Overcoming Barriers:*** Reflect on any hesitations or barriers you've felt towards networking. How can you address and overcome these?

1. ***Continuous Learning:*** Every individual we meet holds a lesson. What have you learned from recent additions to your network, and how can you apply this knowledge moving forward?

As you journey towards expanding your network, may you approach it with a spirit of genuine curiosity, respect, and mutual enrichment. The strength of a network lies not in its numbers but in its depth, diversity, and quality of connections. Embrace each interaction as an opportunity for growth, wisdom, and a step closer to your goals, all while enriching others on their paths.

4

LETTING GO OF TOXIC RELATIONSHIPS

Recognizing Toxic Behaviors

Within the labyrinth of human interactions, there exists a spectrum of behaviors – some nurturing and supportive, while others are damaging and harmful. Recognizing toxic behaviors is essential for our well-being, enabling us to cultivate positive relationships while setting boundaries with those that drain or harm us. Scriptures across various traditions illuminate the characteristics of such behaviors and guide us toward healthier paths.

Supportive Scriptures

1. **Proverbs 22:24-25 (NIV):** "Do not make friends with a hot-tempered person, do not associate with one easily angered, or you may learn their ways and get yourself ensnared." **A warning about the influence of negative behaviors and the risks of association.**

2. **Psalm 1:1 (NIV):** "Blessed is the one who does not walk in step with the wicked or stand in the way that sinners take or sit in the company of mockers." **This verse emphasizes the significance of recognizing and distancing oneself from negative influences.**

3. **Qur'an 25:72 (Islamic scripture):** "And [true servants of the Merciful are] those who do not bear witness to falsehood, and when they

pass by some evil play or evil talk, they pass by it with dignity." **Highlighting the virtue of not engaging with or condoning toxic behavior.**

4. *Romans 12:9 (NIV):* "Love must be sincere. Hate what is evil; cling to what is good." **An encouragement to discern between negative and positive behaviors and to gravitate towards the latter.**

Self-reflection

1. *Patterns of Interactions:* Reflect on your relationships. Are there recurring patterns of negativity, manipulation, or control? How do these patterns affect your well-being?

1. *Emotional Reactions:* Consider times when interactions left you feeling drained, invalidated, or belittled. What behaviors triggered these feelings?

1. *Setting Boundaries:* Think about moments when you've set boundaries to protect yourself from toxic behaviors. How did it impact the relationship, and how did it make you feel?

1. *Personal Accountability:* Are there behaviors or habits you possess that might be perceived as toxic? Reflecting on this can lead to personal growth and better relationships.

1. ***Seeking Counsel:*** Recall instances when you've confided in trusted friends or mentors about certain behaviors you've encountered. How did their perspectives assist in your recognition and handling of toxic situations?

1. ***Root Causes:*** Delve deep and reflect on what might be the root causes of toxic behaviors in those around you. Understanding doesn't mean condoning, but it can lead to empathy and better management of interactions.

1. ***Personal Growth and Learning:*** Think about the lessons you've learned from encountering toxic behaviors. How have these experiences shaped your understanding of relationships and your approach to them?

Recognizing toxic behaviors is the first step in crafting a life surrounded by positivity and genuine connections. May the wisdom of the scriptures guide you in discerning and navigating these challenges. Remember, while we can't control the actions of others, we possess the power to choose our responses, ensuring our peace and well-being.

Assessing the Impact on Your Well-being

Amidst the ebb and flow of life's experiences, our well-being stands as the compass, directing us toward health, balance, and peace. Relationships, environment, choices, and myriad other factors play pivotal roles in influencing this state of harmony. Taking the time to assess their impact—both positive and detrimental—enables proactive steps in nurturing ourselves. Scriptures, spanning various traditions, offer insight into the nature of well-being and the importance of safe-guarding it.

Supportive Scriptures

1. *3 John 1:2 (NIV):* "Dear friend, I pray that you may enjoy good health and that all may go well with you, even as your soul is getting along well." **This verse encapsulates the holistic approach to well-being, emphasizing both physical health and the wellness of the soul.**

2. *Proverbs 17:22 (NIV):* "A cheerful heart is good medicine, but a crushed spirit dries up the bones." **Highlighting the interplay between emotional well-being and physical health.**

3. *Qur'an 2:286 (Islamic scripture):* "...Our Lord! Do not burden us beyond what we have the strength to bear..." **A prayer acknowledging our limitations and seeking balance and endurance.**

4. *Matthew 11:28-30 (NIV):* "Come to me, all you who are weary and burdened, and I will give you rest... For my yoke is easy and my burden is light." **An invitation to find solace and rejuvenation in spiritual connection.**

Self-reflection

1. *Mind, Body, Soul:* Consider the triad of mind, body, and soul. Which areas feel in balance, and which require more attention and care?

1. *Emotional Inventory:* Reflect on the emotions you've predomi-

nantly felt over the past month. Are they indicators of peace and contentment or signals of distress?

1. *Physical Signals:* Our bodies often manifest the impacts of our environment and interactions. Are there recurrent ailments or sensations indicating imbalances in your well-being?

1. *Spiritual Alignment:* Delve into your spiritual state. Do you feel connected, grounded, and in alignment with your beliefs and values?

1. *Environmental Factors:* Think about the places and spaces you frequent. How do they contribute to or detract from your sense of well-being?

1. *Relationship Audit:* Reflect on your close relationships. Which ones uplift and support you, and which might be sources of stress or discomfort?

1. *Rejuvenation and Restoration:* Contemplate the activities and practices that rejuvenate you. Are you making adequate time for these vital restorative moments?

Assessing the impact of external and internal factors on our well-being is akin to tending to a garden. As we recognize which elements nourish and which harm, we can prune, water, and cultivate, ensuring a thriving landscape of health, peace, and vitality. Let the ancient wisdom of scriptures guide you in this introspective journey, illuminating pathways of balance and holistic health.

Setting Boundaries & Communicating Your Needs

Boundaries stand as protective walls around the garden of our well-being. They delineate what we deem acceptable, ensuring that we maintain respect, safety, and care for ourselves and others. Coupled with this is the vital skill of communicating our needs, a dialogue that fosters mutual understanding and harmony in relationships. Scriptures, enriched with timeless wisdom, offer guidance on establishing boundaries and voicing our intrinsic needs.

Supportive Scriptures

1. *Proverbs 4:23 (NIV):* "Above all else, guard your heart, for everything you do flows from it." **This scripture highlights the primacy of protecting one's emotional and spiritual well-being.**

2. *Matthew 5:37 (NIV):* "Let your 'Yes' be 'Yes,' and your 'No' be 'No.'" **An emphasis on clear and unambiguous communication.**

3. *Galatians 6:2 (NIV):* "Carry each other's burdens, and in this way, you will fulfill the law of Christ." **This underscores the significance of understanding and helping with others' needs while balancing our own.**

4. *Qur'an 31:17 (Islamic scripture):* "... And establish the prayer and give the poor-due, and whatever good you send forth for yourselves, you shall find it with Allah..." **A reminder of maintaining our own well-being while also being in service to others.**

Self-reflection

1. *Clarity of Boundaries*: Reflect on areas of your life where boundaries are well-defined, and areas where they might be blurred or non-existent. What might have led to these situations?

1. *Past Experiences:* Think about instances where crossed boundaries resulted in discomfort or distress. What lessons can you derive from these experiences?

1. *Voice and Assertiveness*: Consider moments where you've successfully communicated your needs. How did it feel? Alternatively, reflect on instances where silence or hesitation prevailed. What held you back?

1. *Perceptions and Expectations*: Dive deep into the perception of others' expectations versus your own needs. Is there a balance, or do external expectations often overshadow personal boundaries?

1. *Balancing Empathy and Self-care*: Reflect on your inclination to prioritize others' needs over your own. How can you strike a balance between empathy for others and self-care?

1. ***Seeking Feedback:*** Recall conversations where friends or mentors provided feedback on your communication style. What insights did you gain?

1. ***Visualizing Ideal Interactions:*** Envision a scenario where your boundaries are respected, and your needs met with understanding. What steps can lead you closer to this ideal?

Setting boundaries and communicating needs aren't merely acts of self-preservation. They are profound affirmations of self-respect and mutual regard. As you traverse this path, let the scriptures serve as your compass, guiding you toward interactions steeped in clarity, respect, and mutual understanding. Embrace this journey, for in doing so, you fortify the foundations of lasting, enriching relationships.

Finding Support & Seeking Professional Help

Life, in its grand tapestry of experiences, can present moments of turbulence, uncertainty, and distress. While our internal resilience and the support of loved ones can guide us through many challenges, there are times when seeking professional help becomes not just beneficial, but essential. Sacred scriptures, brimming with insights, remind us of the value of seeking counsel and embracing the support available to us.

Supportive Scriptures

1. ***Proverbs 11:14 (NIV):*** "For lack of guidance a nation falls, but victory is won through many advisers." **This scripture underscores the importance of seeking advice and guidance.**
2. ***Proverbs 19:20 (NIV):*** "Listen to advice and accept discipline, and

in the end, you will be counted among the wise." **A nod to the virtue of seeking and heeding counsel.**

3. *Galatians 6:2 (NIV):* "Bear one another's burdens, and so fulfill the law of Christ." **This suggests that community support and shared understanding are fundamental aspects of our spiritual journey.**

4. *Qur'an 16:43 (Islamic scripture):* "And We sent not before you except men to whom We revealed [Our message]. So, ask the people of the message if you do not know." **An emphasis on seeking knowledge and guidance from those more informed.**

Self-reflection

1. *Recognizing the Need:* Reflect on moments in your life when you felt overwhelmed or stuck. What were the signs that suggested you might benefit from external support?

1. *Barriers to Seeking Help:* Think about any hesitations or barriers that might prevent you from seeking professional assistance. Are they based on past experiences, societal views, or personal beliefs?

1. *Past Experiences with Support:* Recall instances when you sought advice or counseling. What was the outcome, and how did it impact your well-being?

1. ***Identifying Support Systems***: List individuals or organizations you believe could offer support or guidance. This could range from therapists to community support groups.

1. ***Expectations:*** Reflect on what you hope to achieve from professional counseling or support. What would a successful outcome look like to you?

1. ***Empowering Decisions***: Consider moments when you made the empowered decision to prioritize your mental and emotional well-being. How did it shape your subsequent journey?

1. ***Community and Collective Healing***: Ponder over the idea of collective healing—finding support not just individually, but as a community. How can group therapy or community support circles play a role in this?

Finding support and embracing professional help isn't a sign of weakness; rather, it's a testament to one's strength and self-awareness. As the scriptures elucidate, guidance, counsel, and shared burdens have always been instrumental in human progress and well-being. Remember, every step you take toward support is a stride toward a more resilient, balanced, and harmonious self.

Moving Forward & Embracing Positive Connections

Emerging from challenges, acknowledging past pains, and seeking professional help pave the way for a renewed journey. This chapter beckons you to move forward with wisdom, strength, and an open heart, ready to embrace connections that nourish your spirit, mind, and body. Sacred scriptures from various traditions have long celebrated the power of positive connections and the promise of new beginnings.

Supportive Scriptures

1. *Ecclesiastes 3:1 (NIV):* "To everything, there is a season and a time to every purpose under the heaven." **This scripture speaks to the cyclical nature of life and the ever-present opportunity for renewal.**

2. *Philippians 3:13-14 (NIV):* "Brothers and sisters, I do not consider myself yet to have taken hold of it. But one thing I do: Forgetting what is behind and straining toward what is ahead." **A testament to looking forward and pursuing new horizons.**

3. *Isaiah 43:18-19 (NIV):* "Forget the former things; do not dwell on the past. See, I am doing a new thing!" **An affirmation of the potential in every new day and connection.**

4. *Qur'an 94:5-6 (Islamic scripture):* "For indeed, with hardship [will be] ease. Indeed, with hardship [will be] ease." **A reminder of the balance and hope that follows challenges**

Self-reflection

1. *Past Lessons, Future Growth:* Reflect on significant lessons from past relationships and experiences. How can they inform and shape your future connections?

1. ***Vision of Positive Connections:*** Visualize the kind of connections you want to embrace moving forward. What qualities and values do they embody?

1. ***Barriers to New Beginnings:*** Are there any lingering fears, habits, or beliefs that might be obstacles to forging positive connections? How can you address them?

1. ***Re-evaluating Connection Criteria:*** Based on your experiences and growth, define what a 'positive connection' means to you now. How has this definition evolved over time?

1. ***Your Role in Connections:*** Ponder upon the energy and qualities you bring into relationships. How can you contribute to making connections mutually enriching?

1. ***Recognizing and Valuing Growth:*** Celebrate moments when you chose yourself, set boundaries, or made decisions that prioritized your well-being. How did these choices influence your path?

1. ***Affirmations for Moving Forward:*** Craft personal affirmations that resonate with your journey ahead. How can they serve as daily reminders of your goals and aspirations?

Moving forward is a dance of grace and intentionality. Embracing positive connections requires a blend of discernment, vulnerability, and courage. Let the scriptures be your guiding stars, illuminating the path of genuine, heartfelt connections. Remember, every sunrise offers a fresh opportunity, and within each interaction lies the potential for growth, understanding, and boundless love.

5

CULTIVATING POSITIVE RELATIONSHIPS

Self-Reflection & Personal Growth

Self-reflection is akin to the quiet stream of water that reflects the grandeur of the sky and the subtlety of the flora that surrounds it. In its calm depths, truths are unveiled, clarity is attained, and the soul is nurtured. It's in these moments of introspection that one finds the seeds of personal growth. Ancient scriptures from diverse traditions have perennially emphasized the value of introspection and the growth it begets.

Supportive Scriptures

1. *Psalm 139:23-24 (NIV):* "Search me, God, and know my heart; test me and know my anxious thoughts. See if there is any offensive way in me and lead me in the way everlasting." **This verse underscores the desire for divine guidance in self-awareness and correction.**

2. *Lamentations 3:40 (NIV):* "Let us examine our ways and test them and let us return to the LORD." **A call to personal introspection and spiritual alignment.**

3. *2 Corinthians 13:5 (NIV):* "Examine yourselves to see whether

you are in the faith; test yourselves." **An emphasis on personal accountability in one's spiritual journey.**

4. *Qur'an 59:18 (Islamic scripture)*: "O you who have believed, fear Allah and let every soul look to what it has put forth for tomorrow - and fear Allah." **A reminder to be mindful of one's deeds and intentions.**

Self-reflection

1. *Mirror to the Soul*: Reflect on moments when you felt most aligned with your core values. What facilitated this alignment?

1. *Challenges as Catalysts*: Think about challenges that triggered deep introspection. How did these experiences contribute to your personal growth?

1. *Embracing Change*: Consider the changes you've seen in yourself over the past year. Which ones do you cherish, and which ones warrant further reflection?

1. *Acknowledging Blind Spots*: Are there aspects of yourself or your behavior that might remain obscured from your view but are evident to others?

1. ***Patterns in Reflection:*** Identify recurring themes or patterns in your introspective sessions. What do they reveal about your aspirations, fears, or areas of growth?

1. ***Desired Growth Pathways:*** Visualize the facets of personal growth you wish to pursue. What steps can guide you towards these aspirations?

1. ***Sacred Moments of Stillness:*** When and where do you find the most enriching moments of self-reflection? How can you integrate more of these moments into your daily life?

Personal growth is an ongoing journey, and self-reflection is the compass that keeps one oriented toward their true north. As the scriptures reveal, this inward journey is as sacred as the outward experiences of life. In the silent corridors of introspection, one finds the wisdom to evolve, the strength to persevere, and the grace to transform. Embrace this pilgrimage of the soul, for in its depths lies the treasure of authentic personal growth.

Building Trust & Authentic Connections

Trust is the foundation upon which the edifice of genuine connections is built. It is the silent bond that links hearts, fosters understanding, and solidifies relationships. While trust is intangible, its manifestations are profound, deepening the roots of connections and allowing authenticity to flourish. Time-honored scriptures from various traditions touch upon this profound virtue, guiding us on how to nurture it and reap its bountiful rewards.

Supportive Scriptures

1. *Proverbs 3:5-6 (NIV):* "Trust in the LORD with all your heart and lean not on your own understanding; in all your ways submit to him, and he will make your paths straight." **This scripture illuminates the divine aspect of trust.**

2. *1 Corinthians 13:7 (NIV):* "Love always protects, always trusts, always hopes, always perseveres." **A beautiful testament to the inseparable bond between love and trust.**

3. *Psalm 20:7 (NIV):* "Some trust in chariots and some in horses, but we trust in the name of the LORD our God." **An emphasis on the ultimate trustworthiness of the Divine.**

4. *Qur'an 3:159 (Islamic scripture):* "So by mercy from Allah, [O Muhammad], you were lenient with them. And if you had been rude [in speech] and harsh in heart, they would have disbanded from about you." **This verse underscores the value of kindness and understanding in building trust.**

Self-reflection Prompts

1. *Trust in Personal History:* Reflect upon your earliest memories of trust. How were these foundational experiences shaped, and how have they influenced your present perspective?

1. *Challenges to Trust:* Recall a time when your trust was challenged or broken. How did you navigate this, and what did you learn?

1. *Qualities of Trustworthiness:* List the qualities that you believe

define a trustworthy individual. How do you embody these traits in your relationships?

1. ***Symbols of Trust***: What symbols, stories, or metaphors resonate with your understanding of trust? How do they guide your interactions?

1. ***Authenticity and Vulnerability***: Ponder on moments when you've displayed vulnerability in a relationship. How did it influence the depth and authenticity of the connection?

1. ***Building Trust***: Consider practical steps you can undertake to build or rebuild trust in a relationship. What do these reveal about your values and expectations?

1. ***Trust in Self***: How do you nurture trust in yourself and your judgments? Reflect upon moments when this self-trust guided you through uncertainties.

In the realm of human connections, trust is both the cornerstone and the crowning glory. As the scriptures suggest, it's not merely a human virtue but a divine principle that guides our interactions and relationships. Nurturing trust and forging authentic connections is a journey of patience, understanding, and unwavering faith. As you traverse this path, may your connections be imbued with depth, sincerity, and trust that stands the test of time.

Effective Communication & Active Listening

In the symphony of relationships, effective communication is the melody, and active listening, is the harmony. When both are in sync, relationships flourish, understanding deepens, and the spirit of connection thrives. To communicate is human, but to do so with intention, clarity, and empathy is divine. Ancient scriptures from diverse traditions highlight the significance of right speech and the art of listening, reminding us that these are not just interpersonal skills, but spiritual practices.

Supportive Scriptures

1. *Proverbs 18:21 (NIV):* "The tongue has the power of life and death, and those who love it will eat its fruit." **This verse accentuates the potent influence of our words.**

2. *James 1:19 (NIV):* "My dear brothers and sisters, take note of this: Everyone should be quick to listen, slow to speak and slow to become angry." **A foundational principle highlighting the importance of listening before speaking.**

3. *Ephesians 4:29 (NIV):* "Do not let any unwholesome talk come out of your mouths, but only what is helpful for building others up according to their needs, that it may benefit those who listen." **A guideline for constructive communication.**

4. *Qur'an 49:11 (Islamic scripture):* "O you who have believed, let not a people ridicule [another] people; perhaps they may be better than them." **An urge to be mindful and respectful in speech.**

Self-reflection Prompts

1. *Listening to Understand*: Reflect on a recent conversation. Were you fully present, or were you formulating your response while the other person was still speaking?

1. *Silent Spaces*: Think about moments when silence spoke louder than words. How can silence enhance understanding and deepen connections?

1. *Clarity in Expression*: Recall a time when you wished you had communicated more clearly. What would you change if given another chance?

1. *Barriers to Listening*: Identify personal barriers that occasionally hinder your ability to listen actively. Is it distraction, impatience, or a preconceived notion?

1. *Non-verbal Communication*: Reflect on the non-verbal cues you often use or receive. How do they enrich or impede understanding?

1. *Feedback as a Gift*: Think about a piece of feedback you received that was tough to hear but beneficial in the long run. How did it impact your growth?

1. ***Communicating with Empathy***: Consider moments when you communicated with deep empathy. How did it transform the interaction and its outcome?

Effective communication is a dance of words and silences, balanced beautifully by the art of active listening. As the scriptures illuminate, our words carry weight, and our ears are gateways to understanding. To truly communicate is to share a part of oneself, to listen is to receive a part of another. In this sacred exchange, may you find clarity, connection, and the profound joy of being truly understood and understanding in return.

Listening to Respond & Not to React

In the intricate streams of human interactions, there exists a subtle yet transformative distinction: the difference between responding and reacting. While reactions are instantaneous, often fueled by emotions or preconceptions, responses are thoughtful, measured, and grounded in attentive listening. To listen with the intention to respond means to fully absorb, contemplate, and then articulate. Scriptures across traditions have shed light on the wisdom of temperance, understanding, and right speech, guiding us toward the path of conscious communication.

Supportive Scriptures

1. ***Proverbs 15:1 (NIV)***: "A gentle answer turns away wrath, but a harsh word stirs up anger." **This verse emphasizes the power of gentle speech and the potential repercussions of impulsive reactions.**
2. ***James 1:19-20 (NIV)***: "Know this, my beloved brothers: let every person be quick to hear, slow to speak, slow to anger; for the

anger of man does not produce the righteousness of God." **A reminder of the virtues of patience and the value of taking time to respond.**

3. *Proverbs 17:27 (NIV):* "Whoever restrains his words has knowledge, and he who has a cool spirit is a man of understanding." **A testament to the wisdom found in measured speech and composure.**

4. *Qur'an 16:125 (Islamic scripture):* "Invite to the way of your Lord with wisdom and good instruction and argue with them in a way that is best." **Encouragement to approach discussions with wisdom and grace.**

Self-reflection

1. *In the Heat of the Moment:* Reflect on a recent interaction where you reacted rather than responded. What triggered this, and how might you handle a similar situation differently in the future?

1. *Time as an Ally:* Recall a situation where taking a pause before responding proved beneficial. How did the delay change your perspective or your words?

2. *Understanding Over Assumptions:* Think about a time during a conversation when you made an assumption, and it led to a misunderstanding. How can active listening prevent such assumptions?

1. *Emotions and Words:* Consider moments when strong emotions influence your reactions. How can you create a mental space between emotions and articulation?

2. ***Empathy in Listening:*** Reflect on conversations where you felt deeply understood. What aspects of the other person's listening made you feel valued?

1. ***Seeking Clarity:*** How often do you ask clarifying questions in a conversation, ensuring you fully grasp the other person's viewpoint before responding?

1. ***Mindfulness in Conversation:*** How can practices like mindfulness or meditation enhance your ability to listen actively and respond rather than react?

To listen with the intent to genuinely understand and then to respond with grace and clarity is an art—one that enriches conversations, bridges gaps, and nurtures connections. As the scriptures elucidate, our words have power, and with that power comes the responsibility of choice. Choose to respond, choose to understand, and let every conversation be a testament to the depth of your presence and the breadth of your compassion.

Resolving Conflicts & Nurturing Relationships

Conflict, a natural facet of human interactions, is often viewed with apprehension. Yet, if navigated with wisdom, patience, and empathy, conflicts can become catalysts for growth, fostering deeper understanding and strengthening the bonds of relationships. History and spiritual traditions have consistently emphasized the value of reconciliation and the beauty of unity. Scriptures from different corners of the world provide profound insights into handling disputes with grace, guiding souls toward harmony.

Supportive Scriptures

1. *Matthew 5:9 (NIV):* "Blessed are the peacemakers, for they will be called children of God." **This verse underscores the divine favor of those who endeavor to cultivate peace.**

2. *Colossians 3:13 (NIV):* "Bear with each other and forgive one another if any of you has a grievance against someone. Forgive as the Lord forgave you." **A call for forgiveness, reminiscent of the boundless mercy shown by the Divine.**

3. *Proverbs 15:18 (NIV):* "A hot-tempered person stirs up conflict, but the one who is patient calms a quarrel." **Wisdom emphasizes patience as an antidote to discord.**

4. *Qur'an 41:34 (Islamic scripture):* "Good and evil are not alike. Repel [evil] with what is better, and then he, between whom and you there was enmity, will become as though he was a devoted friend." **An inspiring perspective on transforming relationships through kindness.**

Self-reflection

1. *The Root of Conflict:* Reflect on a recent conflict in your life. What do you believe was its underlying cause? Was it miscommunication, differing values, or perhaps unmet expectations?

1. *Responses to Conflict:* How do you typically respond to disagreements? Do you approach them head-on, avoid them, or seek mediation?

2. *Forgiveness:* Think about a time when you found it challenging

to forgive. What emotions held you back, and what eventually helped you move forward?

1. ***Empathy in Resolution:*** Consider a conflict that was resolved through mutual understanding. How did empathy play a role in this resolution?

1. ***Learning from Disagreements:*** Can you recall a disagreement that led to personal growth or a positive change in your relationship? What lessons did it offer?

1. ***Seeking Middle Ground:*** Reflect on a time when compromise paved the way for conflict resolution. How did both parties arrive at this middle ground?

1. ***Reconciliation:*** Think about a relationship that weathered a storm of conflict and emerged stronger. How was reconciliation achieved, and how did it affect the relationship's dynamic?

Conflicts, while challenging, are also opportunities—doorways to deeper understanding, empathy, and mutual growth. As the scriptures remind us, the path of peace, forgiveness, and reconciliation is one of spiritual elevation. Every relationship, like a garden, requires tending. Through understanding and conscious effort, may the flowers of trust and love bloom in your garden, and may the weeds of discord find no ground to root.

6

THE POWER OF DIVERSITY IN YOUR NETWORK

Embracing Differences & Expanding Perspectives

At the heart of human existence lies the captivating tapestry of diversity. Cultures, beliefs, values, and experiences, all so varied yet interconnected, are threads that weave our shared narrative. Embracing these differences is more than just a call for tolerance; it's an invitation to expand our perspectives, enrich our understanding, and truly celebrate the spectrum of humanity. Scriptures, revered reservoirs of wisdom, have often encouraged acceptance and the seeking of knowledge, urging us to venture beyond the familiar and into the realm of expansive understanding.

Supportive Scriptures

1. ***Romans 14:1 (NIV):*** "Accept the one whose faith is weak, without quarreling over disputable matters." **A plea for understanding and acceptance, regardless of varying levels of belief or understanding.**
2. *1 Corinthians 12:4-6 (NIV):* "There are different kinds of gifts, but the same Spirit distributes them. There are different kinds of service, but the same Lord. There are different kinds of working, but in all of them and in everyone it is the same God at work."

An acknowledgment of the diverse ways in which the Divine manifests in our lives.

3. *Proverbs 19:20 (NIV):* "Listen to advice and accept instruction, that you may gain wisdom in the future." **Encouragement to remain open to diverse viewpoints and teachings.**

4. *Qur'an 49:13 (Islamic scripture):* "O mankind, indeed We have created you from male and female and made you peoples and tribes that you may know one another. Indeed, the most noble of you in the sight of Allah is the most righteous of you." **A profound affirmation of diversity to foster understanding and camaraderie among humankind.**

Self-reflection

1. *Beyond the Familiar:* Reflect on a moment when you stepped out of your comfort zone to learn about a culture or belief different from your own. What insights did this experience offer?

1. *Challenging Stereotypes:* Can you recall a time when your preconceived notions about a group or individual were challenged? How did it reshape your understanding?

1. *Growth through Diversity:* Consider the diverse individuals in your life. How have their perspectives and experiences enriched your own journey?

1. ***Bridging Gaps:*** Reflect on an instance when embracing differences led to a deeper connection or the resolution of a misunderstanding.

1. ***Expanding the Horizon:*** Think about a book, movie, or conversation that expanded your perspective on a global issue or culture.
2. *Shared Humanity:* Amidst all the differences, can you identify universal values or emotions that bind us all?

1. ***The Power of Curiosity:*** How often do you find yourself genuinely curious about the worldviews of others? How can this curiosity be a pathway to understanding?

Diversity, in its myriad forms, is one of the universe's most beautiful compositions. By embracing these differences, we not only celebrate the vastness of human experience but also uncover deeper layers of our own understanding. As the scriptures guide and life experiences teach, the journey of expanding perspectives is both enlightening and humbling. May your path be adorned with the colors of diversity, and may every step be a stride towards broader horizons and deeper connections.

Breaking Stereotypes & Challenging Bias

Stereotypes and biases, often deeply ingrained and unchallenged, can subtly shape our thoughts, beliefs, and actions. Whether inherited from cultural narratives, past experiences, or societal norms, they form invisible barriers that hinder true understanding and genuine interactions. Challenging these biases and breaking free from limiting stereotypes is not just an individual endeavor; it's a collective responsibility that paves the way for a more inclusive and compassionate society. Scriptures, timeless in their wisdom, have consistently advocated for fairness, equality, and the inherent dignity of all individuals.

Supportive Scriptures

1. *Acts 10:34-35 (NIV):* "Then Peter began to speak: 'I now realize how true it is that God does not show favoritism but accepts from every nation the one who fears him and does what is right.'" **A revelation about the universality of God's love and acceptance, transcending human-created divisions.**

2. *Galatians 3:28 (NIV):* "There is neither Jew nor Gentile, neither slave nor free, nor is there male and female, for you are all one in Christ Jesus." **A powerful assertion of the inherent equality of all individuals in the eyes of God.**

3. *James 2:9 (NIV):* "But if you show favoritism, you sin and are convicted by the law as lawbreakers." **A warning against the perils of prejudice and bias.**

4. *Qur'an 30:22 (Islamic scripture):* "And among His Signs is the creation of the heavens and the earth, and the difference of your languages and colors. Verily, in that are indeed signs for those who know." **An acknowledgment of the beauty in diversity and the divine intention behind it.**

Self-reflection

1. *Origins of Belief:* Consider the stereotypes or biases you hold. Where did they originate from? Was it from family, society, media, or personal experiences?

1. ***Consequences of Bias***: Reflect on a time when your biases influenced a decision or interaction. What were the consequences?

1. ***Breaking the Mold***: Can you recall an instance when someone defied your stereotypical expectations? How did it make you feel and what did you learn?

1. ***The Power of Stories***: Think about a book, film, or personal narrative that challenged your existing beliefs or biases. How did it reshape your perspective?

1. ***Moments of Realization***: Were there moments in your life that served as wake-up calls to confront your own biases? Describe the feelings and revelations from those moments.

1. ***The Journey of Unlearning***: Reflect on the steps you've taken or plan to take in your journey to unlearn stereotypes and challenge biases.

1. ***Empathy as a Tool***: How can placing yourself in another's shoes help in understanding their perspective and challenging your own biases?

To rise above stereotypes and biases is to see the world with clear eyes, to recognize the intricate dance of individuality and shared humanity. As scriptures remind us, every soul is unique yet united in its quest for understanding, love, and divine connection. By confronting our own biases, we not only liberate ourselves but also play a part in creating a world where every individual is seen, heard, and valued. In this ongoing journey, may your heart remain open, your mind receptive, and your spirit always aligned with the virtues of equity and compassion.

Learning From Different Experiences & Knowledge

In the interconnectedness of human existence, every individual thread tells a unique story. These stories, woven together, form the collective narrative of our species. Our journeys are distinct, and our experiences vary, yet the lessons they offer are universally relevant. By opening ourselves to different perspectives and knowledge systems, we not only enrich our understanding but also foster a spirit of unity and shared growth. Scriptures, repositories of timeless wisdom, emphasize the significance of gaining knowledge, appreciating diversity, and learning from every corner of the earth.

Supportive Scriptures

1. *Proverbs 1:5 (NIV):* "Let the wise listen and add to their learning, and let the discerning get guidance." **An invitation to always remain open to new wisdom, regardless of how much we think we know.**

2. *Proverbs 18:15 (NIV):* "The heart of the discerning acquires knowledge, for the ears of the wise seek it out." **A reminder that the pursuit of knowledge is a continual process.**

3. *Romans 15:4 (NIV):* "For everything that was written in the past was written to teach us, so that through the endurance taught

in the Scriptures and the encouragement they provide we might have hope." **An acknowledgment of the lessons history offers.**

4. *Qur'an 39:9 (Islamic scripture):* "Are those equal, those who know and those who do not know?" **A prompt to recognize the value of knowledge and its role in elevating our existence.**

5. *Qur'an 29:20 (Islamic scripture):* "Say, 'Travel through the land and observe how He began creation. Then Allah will produce the final creation. Indeed Allah, over all things, is competent.'" **An encouragement to learn from observing the world and understanding the diversity of creation.**

Self-reflection

1. *A Different Perspective:* Recall an instance where learning about a different culture or perspective deeply impacted or changed your viewpoint.

1. *Books as Bridges:* Think of a book from a foreign culture or background that opened your eyes to new ideas. What were the main takeaways?

1. *Interactions and Insights:* Reflect on a conversation with someone from a different background. What did you learn, and how did it enrich your understanding?

1. *Challenges in Acceptance:* Were there moments when accepting a different viewpoint was challenging? How did you navigate this?

1. *Lessons from History:* Consider historical events or figures that offer valuable lessons applicable today. How can you incorporate this learning into your life?

1. *Diverse Knowledge Systems:* Reflect on the diverse ways of knowing and understanding the world, such as indigenous knowledge or alternative philosophies. How can these enrich our modern understanding?

1. *The Spirit of Inquiry:* How often do you seek out information or perspectives different from your own? How can you cultivate a more inquisitive mindset?

Life, in its myriad manifestations, offers lessons at every turn. From the distant lands to our own neighborhoods, from ancient scriptures to modern narratives, there's a wealth of knowledge waiting to be tapped. By appreciating the vastness of human experience and remaining open to its lessons, we not only enrich our own journeys but also contribute to the collective wisdom of humanity. As you continue this path of discovery, may every encounter offer insights and every story bring closer the shared dream of understanding and unity.

Creating Inclusive Spaces & Opportunities

In a world abundant with diversity, inclusion becomes a touchstone of community strength. Every person, regardless of background, deserves the chance to shine, to contribute, and to feel welcomed. Yet, many a time, biases — both subtle and explicit — can exclude individuals from opportunities and safe spaces. Creating environments that embrace everyone not only stands as a moral duty but also adds to the richness and depth of shared experiences. The divine teachings enshrined in scriptures call us to love, include, and uplift one another, reminding us that every soul has inherent value.

Supportive Scriptures

1. *Leviticus 19:34 (NIV):* "The foreigner residing among you must be treated as your native-born. Love them as yourself, for you were foreigners in Egypt. I am the LORD your God." **This scripture teaches us the value of treating every individual, regardless of their origin, with love and respect.**

2. *1 Corinthians 12:12-27 (NIV):* An extended passage describing the body's many parts, emphasizing that every part, no matter how seemingly insignificant, is crucial for the whole. **It illustrates the importance of every member of a community.**

3. *Qur'an 49:11 (Islamic scripture):* "O believers! Let not men mock other men, perhaps they may be better than them, nor let women mock other women, perhaps they may be better than them." **Teaching that underscores respect for every individual.**

4. *Galatians 3:28 (NIV):* "There is neither Jew nor Gentile, neither slave nor free, nor is there male and female, for you are all one in Christ Jesus." **A reminder of the intrinsic value of every soul and the unity that binds us all.**

Self-reflection

1. *Spaces of Belonging:* Reflect on a time when you felt completely included or excluded in a space. What elements or actions contributed to those feelings?

1. *Actions over Words:* Think about a time when your actions (or inactions) might have inadvertently excluded someone. How can you ensure such an oversight doesn't happen again?

1. *Cultural Awareness:* How do you educate yourself about cultures, traditions, or practices different from your own? Are there moments when such knowledge helped create a more inclusive space?

1. *Beyond Tokenism:* Reflect on instances where inclusivity might have been mere tokenism rather than genuine inclusion. How can we ensure authenticity in our inclusive efforts?

1. *Listening to Voices:* Recall a time when listening to someone from a marginalized group broadened your understanding of inclusion. What steps did you take afterward?

1. *Opportunities for All:* Think about any barriers that might exist in your community or organization that hinder certain groups from

accessing opportunities. How can you play a role in dismantling such barriers?

1. ***Feedback and Growth:*** Consider seeking feedback on how inclusive your spaces or initiatives truly are. What steps can you take based on the feedback received?

Inclusivity isn't a mere checkbox; it's a heartfelt commitment to ensuring that everyone feels seen, valued, and empowered. As we strive to create spaces that embody these values, it's essential to continuously educate ourselves, challenge our biases, and listen to those who've often been left in the margins. Through genuine efforts and the guiding wisdom of scriptures, we can build communities where every individual thrives and where diversity is celebrated as our collective strength.

Celebrating Diversity & Cultural Exchange

Our world is a beautiful weaving of cultures, traditions, languages, and perspectives. Everyone, with their unique background, adds a vibrant tile to this magnificent tree of life. By celebrating diversity and fostering cultural exchange, we not only show respect and appreciation for the richness around us but also allow our minds and hearts to expand beyond familiar horizons. Spiritual scriptures, which often emphasize unity, love, and respect, serve as powerful reminders that while we may walk different paths, our shared humanity binds us together.

Supportive Scriptures

1. ***Revelation 7:9 (NIV):*** "After this I looked, and there before me was a great multitude that no one could count, from every nation,

tribe, people and language, standing before the throne and before the Lamb." **A vision of universal unity, where all distinctions melt away in divine reverence.**

2. *Qur'an 49:13 (Islamic scripture):* "O mankind, indeed We have created you from male and female and made you peoples and tribes that you may know one another. Indeed, the most noble of you in the sight of Allah is the most righteous of you." **An affirmation that diversity is divinely ordained, and the essence of these differences is to foster mutual understanding.**

3. *Acts 17:26-27 (NIV):* "From one man he made all the nations, that they should inhabit the whole earth; and he marked out their appointed times in history and the boundaries of their lands. God did this so that they would seek him and perhaps reach out for him and find him." **A testament to the unity in creation, highlighting the divine intent behind our diverse manifestations.**

4. *Bhagavad Gita 4:7-8 (Hindu scripture):* "Whenever there is a decline in righteousness and an increase in unrighteousness, O Arjuna, at that time I manifest myself on earth." **This scripture reminds us that divine intervention and teachings manifest across different cultures and eras, celebrating the universality of spiritual truths.**

Self-reflection

1. *Memorable Exchange:* Recall a particularly memorable cultural exchange experience. How did it enrich your perspective or challenge your preconceived notions?

1. *Unknown Traditions:* Think of a tradition or practice from another culture that you find intriguing. How can you respectfully learn more about it?

2. ***Shared Values***: Reflect on common values or themes you've observed across different cultures. How do these shared values shape your understanding of human interconnectedness?

1. ***Overcoming Stereotypes***: Can you remember a time when engaging with someone from a different culture helped debunk a stereotype or bias you held?

1. ***Festivities and Celebrations***: Have you participated in a celebration from a culture other than your own? Describe the experience and its impact on you.

1. ***Language and Communication***: Ponder upon the power of language in bridging gaps. Have you ever tried learning a new language or dialect to connect better with a different community?

1. ***Active Participation***: How do you actively promote and participate in cultural exchange within your community or circles?

To truly celebrate diversity, we must approach cultural exchange with an open heart and genuine curiosity. The world's myriad cultures offer a wealth of knowledge, wisdom, and beauty. By immersing ourselves in this richness, we not only gain a deeper understanding of others but also of ourselves. Let the scriptures guide us in recognizing the divine hand in the vast tapestry of human existence and inspire us to cherish every thread that makes it whole.

7

NAVIGATING PROFESSIONAL RELATIONSHIPS

Networking for Professional Growth

In the journey of professional advancement, technical prowess, and individual talent are undoubtedly essential. Still, they often need to be complemented by the right connections, opportunities, and shared wisdom. Networking is not merely about exchanging business cards; it's about building meaningful relationships that foster mutual growth, collaboration, and mentorship. Scriptures, with their timeless wisdom, remind us that connections, camaraderie, and counsel from others play a pivotal role in one's path to success.

Supportive Scriptures

1. *Proverbs 15:22 (NIV):* "Plans fail for lack of counsel, but with many advisers, they succeed." **This verse accentuates the value of seeking advice and insights from others.**

2. *Ecclesiastes 4:9-10 (NIV):* "Two are better than one, because they have a good return for their labor: If either of them falls down, one can help the other up." **A testament to the strength derived from collaboration and mutual support.**

3. *Proverbs 27:17 (NIV):* "As iron sharpens iron, so one person

sharpens another." **This scripture emphasizes the mutual benefit and growth derived from engaging with peers.**

4. *1 Corinthians 12:21 (NIV):* "The eye cannot say to the hand, 'I don't need you!' And the head cannot say to the feet, 'I don't need you!'" **A reminder of the interdependent nature of community and the unique value each person brings.**

Self-reflection

1. *First Impressions:* Think back to a networking event or situation. What impression did you leave, and how did others perceive you? What would you do differently next time?

1. *Meaningful Connections:* Reflect on the most valuable professional connection you've made. What made this relationship fruitful, and how can you forge more of such connections?

1. *Active Listening:* During networking, are you more of a talker or a listener? How can you balance sharing about yourself while also genuinely learning about others?

1. *Beyond Business:* Networking is not just about professional gain. Can you recall a connection that transcended professional boundaries and turned into a genuine friendship or mentorship?

1. ***Offering Value:*** How often do you approach networking with the mindset of what you can offer rather than what you can gain? What unique value or insight can you bring to your professional circle?

1. ***Expanding Circles:*** Do you find yourself networking within the same circles? How can you diversify and expand your professional network?

1. ***Following Up:*** How consistent are you in following up after initial networking interactions? Reflect on ways to maintain and nurture connections over time.

Networking, when approached with authenticity and a genuine desire to connect, can be a powerful tool for professional growth. It's not just about ascending the corporate ladder but also about growth, collaboration, and mutual upliftment. Scriptures remind us of the value of community, counsel, and collaboration, urging us to engage, connect, and grow together in our professional endeavors.

Building a Personal Brand & Reputation

In an age where individuality is celebrated and digital footprints are increasingly influential, your personal brand and reputation become invaluable assets. But what truly is a personal brand? It's the unique amalgamation of your skills, values, passions, and the impression you leave on others. While technology may have modernized the concept, scriptures have long emphasized the importance of authenticity, integrity, and the lasting mark one leaves on the world.

Supportive Scriptures

1. *Proverbs 22:1 (NIV):* "A good name is more desirable than great riches; to be esteemed is better than silver or gold." **This highlights the lasting value of reputation over transient material wealth.**

2. *Matthew 5:16 (NIV):* "In the same way, let your light shine before others, that they may see your good deeds and glorify your Father in heaven." **A call to lead by example and showcase your authentic self for the betterment of the community.**

3. *Philippians 4:8 (NIV):* "Finally, brothers and sisters, whatever is true, whatever is noble, whatever is right, whatever is pure, whatever is lovely, whatever is admirable—if anything is excellent or praiseworthy—think about such things." **A guide on where to focus your energies and aspirations in building your personal brand.**

4. *1 Peter 2:12 (NIV):* "Live such good lives among the pagans that, though they accuse you of doing wrong, they may see your good deeds and glorify God on the day he visits us." **An encouragement to maintain integrity even amidst skepticism or criticism.**

Self-reflection

1. *Unique Value Proposition:* What unique qualities or experiences differentiate you from others in your field or community? How do you showcase these attributes in your personal and professional life?

1. *Consistency Check:* Reflect on instances where you might have been inconsistent in your actions, words, or online presence. How can you ensure consistency in building your personal brand?

1. *Feedback Receptive:* How often do you seek feedback about your personal brand or reputation? Are there trusted mentors or peers who can provide you with honest insights?

1. *Legacy Pondering:* If people were to describe you in a sentence, what would you want that to be? Does your current reputation align with this desired legacy?

1. *Digital Footprint:* Examine your online presence across platforms. Does it accurately reflect who you are and what you stand for?

1. *Continuous Growth:* In what areas can you further develop or refine your personal brand? Are there skills or experiences you wish to acquire to bolster your reputation?

1. *Values Alignment:* Are your actions, both online and offline, in alignment with your core values and beliefs? If not, what changes can you implement?

Building a personal brand and reputation is an ongoing journey, shaped by consistent actions, continuous learning, and unwavering authenticity. As scriptures highlight, the weight of a good name and genuine deeds surpasses fleeting accolades or riches. In the interconnected world of today, investing in your personal brand is not just a professional necessity but also a testament to your commitment to values, growth, and authentic leadership.

Collaborating & Mentoring in the Workplace

The essence of any thriving workplace lies in its ability to foster collaboration and offer avenues for mentoring. While new tools and technologies emerge to make teamwork more efficient, the age-old principles of mutual respect, understanding, and guidance stand firm. Scriptures have often provided insights into the importance of collective growth, emphasizing the shared journey of enlightenment.

Supportive Scriptures

1. *Ecclesiastes 4:9-10 (NIV):* "Two are better than one, because they have a good return for their labor: If either of them falls down, one can help the other up." **This verse reinforces the strength found in numbers and the support system a collaborative environment fosters.**

2. *Proverbs 27:17 (NIV):* "As iron sharpens iron, so one person sharpens another." **Here, the Bible beautifully depicts how mutual growth and improvement arise from interpersonal interactions.**

3. *1 Thessalonians 5:11 (NIV):* "Therefore encourage one another and build each other up, just as in fact you are doing." **A reminder of the critical role of encouragement and mentorship in any setting.**

4. *Hebrews 10:24 (NIV):* "And let us consider how we may spur one another on toward love and good deeds." **This scripture emphasizes the essence of pushing colleagues towards their potential.**

Self-reflection

1. **Mutual Growth**: Reflect on a moment when collaboration led to

a solution or innovation that wouldn't have been possible individually. What lessons did you learn from this?

1. *Guiding Light*: Can you recall an instance when a mentor or colleague's advice profoundly influenced your professional decisions? How can you pay this guidance forward?
2. *Collaborative Challenges*: While teamwork often yields results, it might come with challenges. Reflect on a challenging collaborative experience. What could have been done differently?

1. *Mentorship Role*: Think about your role as a mentor. Are there colleagues or juniors you can guide? How can you be more accessible to them?

1. *Active Listening in Collaboration:* In team settings, do you actively listen to others' inputs, or are you preoccupied with your perspective? How can you enhance your listening skills?

1. *Openness to Feedback*: Mentorship often involves giving and receiving feedback. How receptive are you to constructive criticism?

1. *Shared Successes*: Can you think of a project where the success was largely due to collaborative efforts? How did you celebrate these shared successes?

Collaboration and mentoring aren't mere workplace strategies; they're vital components for personal growth and organizational success. As scriptures suggest, it's in our collective strength and shared wisdom that we find progress. In fostering an environment where collaboration is celebrated and mentoring is integral, workplaces not only enhance productivity but also nurture a culture of mutual respect, growth, and continuous learning.

Dealing With Difficult Colleagues & Conflict Resolution

At some point in our professional journey, we all face the challenge of dealing with difficult colleagues. The complexities of human nature and the multitude of personalities in the workplace ensure that conflicts are inevitable. However, how we handle these conflicts determines the harmony of our work environment and, ultimately, our own peace of mind. Scriptures offer profound wisdom on managing disagreements, underscoring the importance of patience, understanding, and love.

Supportive Scriptures

1. *Proverbs 15:1 (NIV):* "A gentle answer turns away wrath, but a harsh word stirs up anger." **This reminds us of the power of measured responses and the significance of tone in communication.**
2. *Matthew 18:15-17 (NIV):* "If your brother or sister sins, go and point out their fault, just between the two of you. If they listen to you, you have won them over." **This advocates for direct, private communication to address issues.**
3. *Romans 12:18 (NIV):* "If it is possible, as far as it depends on you, live at peace with everyone." **Emphasizing our personal responsibility in maintaining peace.**
4. *Colossians 3:13 (NIV):* "Bear with each other and forgive one another if any of you has a grievance against someone. Forgive as

the Lord forgave you." **A call to empathy and the higher road of forgiveness.**

Self-reflection

1. *Understanding Triggers:* Reflect on a recent workplace conflict. Were there specific triggers that escalated the situation? How can you navigate or mitigate these triggers in the future?

1. *Active Listening:* During disagreements, do you genuinely listen to the other person's viewpoint, or are you formulating your response? How can you cultivate a habit of true active listening?

1. *Empathy Exercise:* Put yourself in the shoes of a difficult colleague. Can you identify any external pressures or personal challenges they might be undergoing? How does this shift your perspective of their behavior?

1. *Response Mechanism:* Think about how you typically respond to conflicts. Are you defensive, aggressive, passive, or assertive? How can you work towards a more balanced response mechanism?

1. *Seeking Mediation:* Are there situations where seeking a neutral third party or HR's intervention might be beneficial for conflict resolution?

1. ***Growth from Conflict:*** Every conflict offers a learning opportunity. Can you think of a past disagreement that, in hindsight, spurred personal or professional growth?

1. ***Scriptural Guidance:*** Reflect on the scriptures provided. Which one resonates most with your current challenges in the workplace? How can its teachings be applied?

Dealing with difficult colleagues and conflicts is a test of character, patience, and resilience. As scriptures suggest, the path to resolution is often paved with understanding, direct communication, and the will to maintain harmony. By continuously reflecting on our actions and seeking divine wisdom, we can transform the challenges of workplace conflicts into opportunities for growth, understanding, and strengthening relationships.

Creating a Supportive Professional Network

In our professional journey, the significance of having a robust and supportive network cannot be overstated. Just as roots nourish a tree, a strong network feeds our career with opportunities, guidance, and resilience. Building a network goes beyond mere transactional relationships; it's about fostering genuine connections, grounded in mutual respect, and understanding. Scriptures provide a timeless perspective on the importance of unity, collective strength, and the mutual support of a community.

Supportive Scriptures

1. *Proverbs 27:9 (NIV):* "Oil and perfume make the heart glad, and the sweetness of a friend comes from his earnest counsel." **This speaks to the enrichment and wisdom that genuine connections can provide.**

2. *Ecclesiastes 4:12 (NIV):* "Though one may be overpowered, two can defend themselves. A cord of three strands is not quickly broken." **Emphasizing the collective strength that arises from unity and collaboration.**

3. *1 Corinthians 12:14 (NIV):* "For the body is not one member, but many." **Reminding us that everyone, with their unique strengths and abilities, contributes to the larger fabric of a supportive community.**

4. *Romans 12:5 (NIV):* "So in Christ, we, though many, form one body, and each member belongs to all the others." **An exhortation to recognize and value the interconnectedness of our professional community.**

Self-reflection

1. *Value Beyond Utility:* Reflect on the essence of your current professional network. Are your connections merely transactional or rooted in mutual respect and understanding?

1. *Genuine Engagement:* When was the last time you reached out to someone in your network without any direct professional motive? How can you engage more authentically?

1. ***Diversifying Your Network:*** Is your network diverse in terms of experience, industry, and perspective? How can you expand your circle to include varied voices?

1. ***Mutual Growth:*** Think of moments when someone from your network aided your professional journey. How can you reciprocate or assist another?

1. ***First Impressions:*** Reflect on your approach to making new connections. Are you open, approachable, and attentive?

1. ***Networking Platforms:*** Are you utilizing the right platforms (both online and offline) to build and nurture your network effectively?

1. ***Guidance from Scriptures:*** Which scripture resonates the most with your networking approach? How can you integrate its wisdom into your networking endeavors?

Crafting a supportive professional network is a continuous journey of genuine interactions, mutual respect, and understanding. As scriptures highlight, there's immense power in unity and collaboration. By reflecting on our networking methods, and seeking divine guidance, we can create a professional circle that's not only beneficial for career growth but also enriching for personal development and well-being.

8

CHAPTER 8: MAINTAINING HEALTHY RELATIONSHIPS

Continuous Communication & Check-ins

In the realm of both professional and personal relationships, the importance of continuous communication cannot be emphasized enough. Just as a plant needs water at regular intervals to thrive, relationships require regular check-ins and communication to flourish. This practice not only nurtures existing bonds but also paves the way for addressing potential issues before they escalate. Scriptures, with their timeless wisdom, elucidate the importance of consistent and genuine communication.

Supportive Scriptures

1. *James 1:19 (NIV):* "My dear brothers and sisters, take note of this: Everyone should be quick to listen, slow to speak, and slow to become angry." **A poignant reminder of the virtues of active listening in communication.**

2. *Proverbs 25:11 (NIV):* "A word fitly spoken is like apples of gold in a setting of silver." **Highlighting the significance of timely and apt communication.**

3. *Ephesians 4:25 (NIV):* "Therefore, having put away falsehood, let

each one of you speak the truth with his neighbor, for we are members one of another." **Advocating for truthfulness and sincerity in our interactions.**

4. *Colossians 4:6 (NIV):* "Let your conversation be always full of grace, seasoned with salt, so that you may know how to answer everyone." **A call to enrich our communication with wisdom and kindness.**

Self-reflection

1. *Frequency of Check-ins:* Reflect on your current communication habits. Are you checking in with your colleagues, friends, or family often enough to understand their needs and sentiments?

1. *Quality over Quantity:* When communicating, is your approach more about the quantity of words or the quality and sincerity of the exchange?

1. *Active Listening:* Do you find yourself truly listening during conversations, or are you often preoccupied with formulating your next response?

1. *Addressing Discomfort:* Think about a recent situation where communication was challenging. How did you navigate it? Was there room for improvement?

1. *Openness to Feedback:* When someone provides feedback or shares a concern, how receptive are you? Do you view it as an opportunity for growth?

1. *Consistency in Words and Actions:* Reflect on whether your actions align with your words. Is there consistency in what you communicate and how you follow through?

1. *Scriptural Alignment:* Which scripture resonates most with your current communication style? How can its teachings influence your future interactions?

Consistent communication and regular check-ins are pivotal in building trust and understanding in relationships. Through genuine interaction, rooted in the principles highlighted by scriptures, we can foster relationships that stand the test of time. Embracing the virtues of active listening, sincerity, and grace ensures that our communication not only maintains connections but also strengthens the bonds of trust and mutual respect.

Adapting to Change & Growth

Change is an inevitable aspect of life, both personally and professionally. It's a force that, at times, sweeps us off our feet, compelling us to adapt and evolve. Growth, too, though often welcomed, comes with its own set of challenges. Our ability to adapt to both change and growth determines our resilience, our potential for success, and our overall well-being. Scriptures, with their profound insights, shed light on the impermanence of life and the virtues of adaptability and embracing growth.

Supportive Scriptures

1. *James 1:2-4 (NIV):* "Consider it pure joy, my brothers and sisters, whenever you face trials of many kinds, because you know that the testing of your faith produces perseverance." **This scripture emphasizes the transformative power of challenges and how they mold our character.**

2. *Proverbs 24:5-6 (NIV):* "A wise man is full of strength, and a man of knowledge enhances his might, for by wise guidance you can wage your war, and in abundance of counselors there is victory." **A reminder that wisdom and adaptability go hand in hand, and seeking guidance in times of change can be invaluable.**

3. *Isaiah 43:19 (NIV):* "Behold, I am doing a new thing; now it springs forth, do you not perceive it? I will make a way in the wilderness and rivers in the desert." **Here, God reassures us that even in times of vast change, new beginnings and pathways can emerge if we remain open and receptive.**

4. *Ephesians 4:22-24 (NIV):* "You were taught, with regard to your former way of life, to put off your old self... and to put on the new self, created to be like God in true righteousness and holiness." **This scripture underlines the continuous cycle of shedding the old and embracing the new that accompanies personal growth.**

Self-reflection

1. *Growth's Discomfort*: Think about a recent period of growth or change in your life. What challenges arose, and how did you navigate them?

1. *Embracing the Unknown*: How comfortable are you with uncertainty? Do you find it exhilarating, daunting, or a mix of both?

1. *Old Habits*: Are there habits or thought patterns that no longer serve your current path or goals? How can you actively work on shedding them?

1. *Seeking Guidance:* When faced with change, do you seek guidance, whether it's from mentors, scriptures, or introspection? How has this helped you adapt?

1. *Visualization:* Imagine yourself a year from now, having successfully adapted to your current challenges. What steps did you take to achieve that vision?

1. *Scriptural Solace:* Which scripture speaks to your heart the most

when navigating change? How can its teachings be applied to your current situation?

Change and growth, though often challenging, offer rich opportunities for self-evolution. As we journey through life's ever-shifting terrains, the scriptures provide solace and guidance, reminding us of the larger tapestry of existence in which change is but a thread. By reflecting, seeking guidance, and embracing the wisdom of scriptures, we can not only adapt to change and growth but also harness them as catalysts for profound personal transformation.

Supporting One Another Goals & Dreams

In the journey of life, while individual ambitions are crucial, mutual support is a foundation upon which great accomplishments can be built. When we uplift those around us, celebrating their aspirations and dreams, we in turn cultivate a community of encouragement and positivity. This spirit of camaraderie, deeply rooted in many scriptural teachings, can be the catalyst for not only achieving our dreams but also contributing to the success of others.

Supportive Scriptures

1. *1 Thessalonians 5:11 (NIV):* "Therefore encourage one another and build each other up, just as in fact you are doing." **This verse reinforces the divine directive of mutual upliftment.**
2. *Hebrews 10:24-25 (NIV):* "And let us consider how we may spur one another on toward love and good deeds, not giving up meeting together, as some are in the habit of doing, but encouraging one another." **A powerful reminder of the collective strength that arises from unity and support.**
3. *Galatians 6:2 (NIV):* "Carry each other's burdens, and in this way,

you will fulfill the law of Christ." **This scripture speaks to the virtue of empathy and the profound act of sharing and alleviating each other's challenges.**

4. *Proverbs 27:17 (NIV):* "As iron sharpens iron, so one person sharpens another." **Highlighting that through mutual support and constructive feedback, we help each other grow and refine our abilities.**

Self-reflection

1. *Reciprocal Support:* Reflect on the last time someone supported your goals. How did it feel? Now, think about the last time you supported someone else's ambitions. How did these experiences differ?

1. *Understanding Dreams:* Do you truly understand the dreams and aspirations of your close friends and family? Have you taken the time to listen and comprehend what drives them?

1. *Shared Success:* Think of a shared victory that you and someone close celebrated. How did mutual support contribute to that success?

1. *Overcoming Differences:* Recall a time when you disagreed with someone's goal or the path they chose. How did you navigate your feelings while still offering support?

1. *Scriptural Reflection:* Which of the above scriptures resonates most with your approach to supporting others? How can its wisdom influence future interactions?

1. *The Power of Encouragement:* Consider the weight of your words and actions. Are they more often encouraging or discouraging to those sharing their dreams with you?

Supporting each other's dreams and ambitions is not merely a kind gesture but a spiritual duty that enriches the collective human experience. By celebrating one another's successes and being a pillar of strength during challenges, we emulate the teachings of scriptures and further the spread of love, understanding, and unity. In this mutual exchange, we find that by lifting others, we too are elevated.

Celebrating Milestones & Expressing Gratitude

In our fast-paced world, pausing to acknowledge our achievements and express gratitude can easily be overlooked. Yet, it is these very acts of recognition and thankfulness that add depth, joy, and a deeper sense of purpose to our lives. Celebrating milestones, whether grand or seemingly small, and cultivating a heart of gratitude are practices profoundly encouraged by scriptures. They remind us of the blessings that abound and inspire us to continue our journey with renewed vigor.

Supportive Scriptures

1. *1 Thessalonians 5:18 (NIV):* "Give thanks in all circumstances; for this is God's will for you in Christ Jesus." This scripture

encourages us to find gratitude in every situation, recognizing the divine will in all experiences.

2. *Psalm 9:1 (NIV):* "I will give thanks to the Lord with my whole heart; I will recount all of your wonderful deeds." A beautiful affirmation of celebrating the countless blessings and moments of divine intervention in our lives.

3. *Colossians 3:15-17 (NIV):* "Let the peace of Christ rule in your hearts... And whatever you do, whether in word or deed, do it all in the name of the Lord Jesus, giving thanks to God the Father through him." A reminder to carry gratitude in our hearts and actions, acknowledging the divine in all we do.

4. *James 1:17 (NIV):* "Every good and perfect gift is from above, coming down from the Father of the heavenly lights." This scripture emphasizes recognizing and celebrating the countless blessings bestowed upon us.

Self-Reflection

1. *Milestones Big and Small:* Reflect on the last milestone you celebrated. Why was it significant, and how did you honor that moment?

1. *Daily Gratitude:* Do you have a daily practice of expressing gratitude? How does this practice influence your perspective on life's challenges and blessings?

1. ***Recognizing Others:*** Think about someone who recently achieved a milestone. Have you taken a moment to congratulate them and share in their joy?

1. ***Hidden Blessings:*** Recall a challenging time in your life. In hindsight, can you identify any blessings or lessons for which you are now grateful?

1. ***Scriptural Inspiration:*** Which of the provided scriptures resonates most deeply with your approach to gratitude and celebration? How can its teachings be more deeply integrated into your daily life?

1. ***The Ripple Effect:*** Consider the impact of expressing gratitude or celebrating someone's achievement on your relationships and community. How do these acts influence the collective energy and spirit?

In every milestone, there lies a story of perseverance, faith, and divine guidance. By celebrating these moments and expressing gratitude, we not only honor our journey but also recognize the greater forces that guide and support us. As scriptures suggest, gratitude and celebration are not just acts of joy, but profound spiritual practices that connect us to the divine and enrich our human experience.

Embracing Forgiveness & Resilience

Life is an intricate meshing of experiences, both uplifting and challenging. Amidst its diverse threads, two essential strands stand out: forgiveness and resilience. Forgiveness allows us to release burdens of the past and grant ourselves and others the freedom to evolve. Resilience, complemented by gratitude, equips us to navigate adversity with strength and grace, consistently rebounding with renewed purpose. These principles, championed in many scriptural teachings, guide us towards inner peace and personal growth.

Supportive Scripture

1. *Ephesians 4:31-32 (NIV):* "Get rid of all bitterness, rage and anger, brawling and slander, along with every form of malice. Be kind and compassionate to one another, forgiving each other, just as in Christ God forgave you." **A direct call to embrace forgiveness as an act of love, mirroring the divine love we receive.**

2. *Proverbs 24:16 (NIV):* "For though the righteous fall seven times, they rise again." **This scripture speaks to the resilient spirit of those who walk a righteous path, emphasizing the importance of perseverance.**

3. *Romans 5:3-4 (NIV):* "Not only so, but we also glory in our sufferings, because we know that suffering produces perseverance; perseverance, character; and character, hope." **An acknowledgment of the transformative power of challenges and the resilience they foster.**

4. *Colossians 3:13 (NIV):* "Bear with each other and forgive one another if any of you has a grievance against someone. Forgive as the Lord forgave you." **This verse serves as a reminder of our divine mandate to forgive, fostering unity and understanding.**

Self-Reflection

1. ***Releasing the Past:*** Reflect upon a past grievance. Have you truly forgiven, or are there residual feelings still lingering?

1. ***Times of Adversity:*** Think about a challenging time in your life. How did resilience play a role in overcoming that challenge? What role did gratitude play in recognizing the strength you gained?

1. ***Lessons in Resilience:*** Recall a situation where you observed resilience in someone else. What did you learn from their approach and attitude?

1. ***The Power of Letting Go:*** Ponder upon the emotional and spiritual liberation experienced when you genuinely forgave someone. How did this act impact your well-being and relationships?

1. ***Scriptural Application:*** Which scripture mentioned above deeply resonates with your personal journey of forgiveness and resilience? How can you further implement its wisdom in your life?

1. ***Resilience and Growth:*** Consider the interplay between resilience and personal growth. How has navigating challenges with a resilient spirit contributed to your evolution?

Embracing forgiveness is akin to unshackling our souls from past pains, granting us and those around us the gift of growth and new beginnings. Complementing this is resilience, a testament to our inner strength, refined and strengthened by life's trials. As scriptures guide us, when combined with gratitude, these principles can pave the path towards a fulfilling, spiritually enriched existence.

9

CHAPTER 9: YOUR INNER CIRCLE AND ITS IMPACT

Evaluating Your Inner Circle

As we journey through life, the company we keep plays a pivotal role in shaping our values, perspectives, and even our destiny. Our inner circle, those closest to us, profoundly influence our behaviors, decisions, and emotions. Thus, periodic evaluations of these relationships are paramount to ensure their alignment with our spiritual and personal growth. Scripture, in its timeless wisdom, offers guiding principles to discern the authenticity and intention of those we let into our sanctum.

Supportive Scriptures

1. *Proverbs 13:20 (NIV):* "He who walks with the wise grows wise, but a companion of fools suffers harm." **A poignant reminder of the influence those around us wield on our character and decisions.**

2. *1 Corinthians 15:33 (NIV):* "Do not be misled: 'Bad company corrupts good character.'" **This scripture provides clear caution about the potential negative impact of unsupportive relationships.**

3. *Proverbs 27:17 (NIV):* "Iron sharpens iron, and one sharpens

another." **Emphasizing the positive, transformative impact of uplifting relationships.**

4. *2 Corinthians 6:14 (NIV):* "Do not be yoked together with unbelievers. For what do righteousness and wickedness have in common? Or what fellowship can light have with darkness?" **A call for discernment in our associations, aligning ourselves with those who share our values.**

Self-reflection

1. *Influence and Alignment:* Reflect on your closest relationships. Do they inspire, uplift, and align with your core values, or do they pull you into negativity and stagnation?

1. *Shared Growth:* Think about a friend or family member in your inner circle. How have you both supported each other's growth and well-being?

1. *Seeking Balance:* Have there been moments when someone in your inner circle was going through a challenging phase, and you provided the necessary support? How did it influence the relationship?

1. *Scriptural Resonance:* Which of the scriptures strongly echoes your current feelings or experiences regarding your inner circle? How might its teachings assist in refining your relationships?

1. ***Drawing Boundaries:*** Consider a time when you had to set boundaries or even distance yourself from someone for your well-being. How did that decision impact your spiritual and emotional health?

1. ***The Circle's Evolution:*** Recognize that as you grow, your inner circle might evolve. Reflect upon how your inner circle has changed over the years and what those changes reveal about your journey.

The people we surround ourselves with have the power to either stifle or amplify our spiritual and personal growth. By mindfully evaluating our inner circle, we can ensure that our relationships not only bring joy and support but also align with our divine path and purpose. As scriptures remind us, being discerning about our associations, while occasionally challenging, is instrumental for a life of wisdom and fulfillment.

Surrounding Yourself with Positive Influencers

The journey of personal growth and spiritual enlightenment is often a reflection of the company we keep. While we remain the primary architects of our destiny, those we surround ourselves with can serve as either catalysts or hindrances to our progress. Just as a single lit candle can illuminate a dark room, aligning with positive influencers can brighten our path, imbuing us with inspiration, motivation, and wisdom. The scriptures, abundant in their wisdom, provide a guiding light on the value of such association.

Supportive Scriptures

1. *Proverbs 12:26 (NIV):* "The righteous choose their friends carefully, but the way of the wicked leads them astray." **This highlights the importance of discernment in our associations.**

2. *Philippians 4:8-9 (NIV):* "Finally, brothers and sisters, whatever is true, whatever is noble, whatever is right, whatever is pure, whatever is lovely, whatever is admirable—if anything is excellent or praiseworthy—think about such things... and the God of peace will be with you." **A call to focus on the positive, which includes our associations.**

3. *Hebrews 10:24-25 (NIV):* "And let us consider how we may spur one another on toward love and good deeds, not giving up meeting together, as some are in the habit of doing, but encouraging one another..." **Emphasizing the positive influence of uplifting relationships.**

4. *1 Thessalonians 5:11 (NIV):* "Therefore encourage one another and build each other up, just as in fact you are doing." **A reminder of the transformative potential of positive relationships.**

Self-reflection

1. *Personal Influence List:* Identify the top five people you spend the most time with. Reflect on how each of them influences your thoughts, actions, and feelings.

1. *Seeking Positivity:* Recall a time when a positive influence significantly impacted a decision or mindset shift in your life. How did their perspective or advice illuminate your situation?

1. ***Scriptural Guidance:*** Which of the provided scriptures resonates the most with your current circle of influencers? How can its teachings guide your future associations?

1. ***Evolving Associations:*** Think about a relationship that transitioned from being negative to positive or vice versa. What caused this shift, and what did you learn from it?

1. ***Qualities of Positive Influencers:*** Reflect on the qualities you value most in positive influencers. Are these attributes currently prevalent in your circle?

1. ***Emulating Positivity:*** Consider how you can become a positive influencer in someone else's life. In what ways can you uplift and inspire others?

Surrounding ourselves with positive influencers is akin to nurturing our souls with the nourishment of encouragement, wisdom, and love. By actively seeking out and valuing these relationships, we not only enrich our own lives but also contribute to the broader collective of growth and spirituality. Let the scriptures serve as our compass, guiding us towards associations that echo divine intentions for our journey.

Supportive Inner Circle for Personal & Professional Growth

In our quest for personal and professional fulfillment, the right company plays a pivotal role. While our individual efforts and ambitions propel us forward, it's often the encouragement, wisdom, and constructive critique of our inner circle that refines and elevates our journey. It's essential to cultivate a circle that not only supports our aspirations but also challenges us, guiding us towards betterment in both personal and professional realms. Scriptures, in their timeless wisdom, reflect on the importance and intricacies of such associations.

Supportive Scriptures

1. *Proverbs 27:17 (NIV):* "As iron sharpens iron, so one person sharpens another." **This verse beautifully captures the essence of mutual growth and the value of constructive relationships.**

2. *Hebrews 10:24 (NIV):* "And let us consider how we may spur one another on toward love and good deeds." **A testament to the transformative power of uplifting relationships in all facets of life.**

3. *1 Corinthians 15:33 (NIV):* "Do not be misled: 'Bad company corrupts good character.'" **A cautionary reminder of the effects our associations can have on our overall character and trajectory.**

4. *Ephesians 4:29 (NIV):* "Do not let any unwholesome talk come out of your mouths, but only what is helpful for building others up according to their needs, that it may benefit those who listen." **This speaks to the responsibility and impact of our words, especially within our inner circle.**

Self-reflection

1. *Balanced Circle:* Reflect on your inner circle. Are there individuals who support your personal dreams as fervently as they provide insights into your professional aspirations? How do they strike this balance?

1. ***Moments of Refinement:*** Recall a situation when a close confidante provided feedback or advice that proved instrumental in your personal or professional growth. What was the outcome?
2. ***Scriptural Alignment:*** Which scripture resonates most with your current inner circle's dynamics? How can its teachings influence your future associations?

1. ***Diverse Insights:*** Consider the diversity of your inner circle in terms of experiences, professions, and perspectives. How has this diversity enriched your personal and professional journey?

1. ***Cherishing Constructive Critique:*** Think of a time when a close individual offered you constructive criticism. How did you respond, and in retrospect, how did it contribute to your growth?

1. ***Nurturing Mutual Growth:*** Reflect on how you've supported someone from your inner circle in their journey. Has their success story inspired your personal or professional endeavors?

Our inner circle often serves as a mirror, reflecting our strengths, potential areas of growth, and the boundless possibilities that lie ahead. By surrounding ourselves with individuals who champion our cause and challenge us to rise higher, we ensure a more holistic growth trajectory. The scriptures emphasize the harmony of such associations and the manifold blessings they bring into our lives. By consciously nurturing these bonds, we pave the way for shared success, growth, and fulfillment.

Investing in Your Inner Circle

Life, with its myriad challenges and blessings, is often made richer by those we journey alongside. The value of our inner circle—those few trusted souls who share our highs and lows—is immeasurable. However, like any significant facet of our lives, these relationships demand intentionality, care, and consistent investment. By committing time, effort, and love to these relationships, we not only fortify our own spiritual and emotional well-being but also contribute to the enrichment of those we hold dear. The scriptures provide profound insights into the depth and significance of such investments.

Supportive Scriptures

1. *Proverbs 17:17 (NIV):* "A friend loves at all times, and a brother is born for a time of adversity." **This scripture speaks to the steadfastness of true friendship and the importance of mutual support.**

2. *Ecclesiastes 4:9-10 (NIV):* "Two are better than one, because they have a good return for their labor: If either of them falls down, one can help the other up. But pity anyone who falls and has no one to help them up." **A testament to the strength and benefit of companionship.**

3. *Romans 12:10 (NIV):* "Be devoted to one another in love. Honor one another above yourselves." **This verse reminds us of the self-less nature of genuine connections.**

4. *1 Thessalonians 5:14 (NIV):* "And we urge you, brothers and sisters, warn those who are idle and disruptive, encourage the disheartened, help the weak, be patient with everyone." **Highlighting the multifaceted roles, we play in the lives of our inner circle.**

Self-reflection

1. *Reciprocal Efforts:* Think of a moment when someone from your inner circle needed you. How did you respond, and how did it strengthen the bond?

1. *Time Investment:* Reflect on the last time you intentionally set aside time for someone close. Was it a deep conversation, a shared activity, or perhaps just silent companionship? How did it nourish the relationship?

1. *Scriptural Resonance:* Which of the scriptures aligns closest with your current efforts in investing in your inner circle? How can its wisdom guide your future interactions?

1. *Cultivating Depth:* Ponder on a relationship within your inner circle that has deepened over time. What mutual investments contributed to its growth?

1. *Moments of Growth:* Think of a challenging time within your inner circle—a disagreement, a hardship, or a misunderstanding. How did you both navigate it and what did you learn?

1. ***The Gift of Presence:*** Reflect on the significance of merely being "present" for someone. How has your undivided attention or presence positively impacted a relationship recently?

Investing in our inner circle is not merely about time; it's about depth, presence, understanding, and mutual growth. As we navigate the ebb and flow of life, the strength and quality of these relationships often become our anchor. With the scriptures as our guide and our hearts as compasses, let's consciously cultivate, cherish, and nourish the invaluable bonds that make our journey meaningful.

Being a Positive Influence in Your Inner Circle

The dynamics of our inner circle aren't just defined by how its members influence us, but also by the kind of influence we exert within it. Being a beacon of positivity, hope, and inspiration within your close-knit group can spark significant transformations. When we uplift, guide, and support those around us, we not only foster a nurturing environment but also find a sense of purpose.